On Ret

CW00554758

This new series, published by Medio Media/Arthur James, responds to the spiritual needs of people living today's busy and stressed lifestyle. Each book in the series is designed to allow the reader to develop a space for silence and solitude and spiritual practice in the context of ordinary life or by taking a short period of withdrawal. The structure of the book allows a flexible time-table to be constructed which integrates periods of reading, physical practice or exercise, and meditation.

John Main was first introduced to meditation in the East. After becoming a Benedictine monk he discovered the Christian tradition of meditation as the 'pure prayer' of the Desert Fathers. His first Christian Meditation Centre, founded at his monastery in London in 1975, led to a community in Canada and, after his death in 1982, to a worldwide community of meditators in the Christian tradition, meeting today in more than a hundred countries.

The 'On Retreat With ...' Series

AWAKENING

On Retreat With
John Main

MEDIO MEDIA / ARTHUR JAMES

LONDON AND BERKHAMSTED

First published in Great Britain in 1997 by

MEDIO MEDIA LTD
in association with
ARTHUR JAMES LTD
70 Cross Oak Road
Berkhamsted
Hertfordshire HP4 3HZ

A catalogue record for this book is available
from the British Library.

Unless otherwise stated, Scripture quotations are from the
New English Bible, copyright © 1970 Oxford University Press
and Cambridge University Press

ISBN 0 85305 424 X

Typeset in Monotype Bulmer by
Strathmore Publishing Services, London N7

Printed and bound in Great Britain by
Guernsey Press Ltd, Guernsey, C.I.

Contents

Being on retreat:
how to do it yourself

Stay in your cell and your cell will teach you everything.
– Saying of the Desert Fathers

The problems of the world arise from people's inability to
sit still in their own room.
– Pascal, *Pensées*

Why set aside time for retreat?
Nature believes in retreats. Each day we virtually shut down our
active processes of mind and body for the retreat and renewal we
call sleep. Each year the animal and vegetable worlds go through
periods of deep rest we call hibernation. These are not escapes
from reality but ways of becoming more deeply attuned to reality,
respecting its ways and trusting the inherent wisdom of nature.

Between each breath there is a moment of cessation, of deep
stillness, which is not the stillness of inaction but the stillness of
non-action. Between periods of daily work we naturally trust the
mind and body when they tell us to rest. Between two thoughts
there is an instant of mental silence.

On the London Underground, many stations have a recorded
announcement each time the train stops, warning passengers step-
ping from the train to the platform to 'mind the gap'. Minding the
gap is what this book is about – helping you, we hope, to see and
respect the natural human need to retreat from action and speech

[7]

at set times so that we can return to speech and action refreshed, re-balanced and renewed.

The spiritual life is not a specialized part of daily life. Everything you do in the day, from washing to eating breakfast, having meetings, driving to work, solving problems, making more problems for yourself once you have solved them, watching television or deciding instead to read, going to a restaurant or a movie or going to church, *everything* you do is your spiritual life. It is only a matter of how consciously you do these ordinary things, how attentive you are to the opportunities they offer for growth, for enjoyment, and how mindfully, how selflessly, how compassionately you perform them. Yet to live life spiritually all the time everyone needs to take specific times to focus on the spiritual dimension before everything else.

'Set your mind on God's kingdom and his justice before everything else, and all the rest will come to you as well.' Jesus said this in his Sermon on the Mount (Matt. 6:33). Taking a time of retreat will help you discover what he means by 'kingdom' and 'justice'. It will teach you that the kingdom is not a place but an experience of presence. The kingdom is within us and all around us. And you will learn that justice means balance, harmony, order. We hunger for justice in all the activities and relationships of our lives.

Buddhists see the spiritual significance of daily life in terms of ordinary mindfulness: doing everything with awareness, wakefulness. Christians similarly have long worked at praying at all times, giving glory to God in everything they do, practising the presence of God. This does not mean going around muttering prayers to yourself all day. You would only be more distracted in what you are doing. Nor does it mean thinking about God all the time. That would make you a religious fanatic. Praying ceaselessly, practising the divine presence is not something extra we do but the way we do whatever we are doing. It is a way of *being* in the midst of action: of being-in-action.

[8]

Perhaps the best comparison is with a relationship with someone you love. The awareness, the mindfulness, of that love surrounds and permeates you and all your words and responses all the day. You do not have to be thinking of the person you love all the time but they are with you and their often silent presence transforms your consciousness. Yet at the end of the day, or whenever opportunity allows, you return to the full presence of that person. Being with them helps the relationship to grow and deepen, even when romance wears thin. The 'quality times' together are essential for the health and development of love.

How to set up a retreat

The 'On Retreat With ...' series has been prepared to help you to spend quality time in the most fundamental relationship of your life, your relationship with God. In the ground of this relationship are planted all your human relationships, even your relationship with yourself. Quality time with someone requires a certain degree of exclusivity – you say *no* to other invitations and pleasant opportunities in order to concentrate on your presence with one person. Other jobs and responsibilities go on hold. When you return to address them you will be refreshed, calmer, and you can see the problems that easily overwhelm you in a better perspective. Retreat is not escape. You make a retreat in order to address reality more realistically and courageously. Retreat does not solve your problems but it helps you deal with them in a more peaceful and hopeful way. This is the meaning of a retreat: we retreat in order to advance deeper into the mystery of love's reality.

This book can help you structure your time and set the tone for the period of retreat you are allowing yourself to take. As life today is very busy and as it often seems impossible to find time for silence, stillness, and non-action, we need all the help we can get in order to take the time of spiritual retreat which both spiritual and psychological health require.

Time and place: your cell

You do not need to take a great stretch of time to make a retreat. But you need to designate a certain period of time and stick to it. It could be an hour, a morning or afternoon, a day, a weekend, a week, three months. In some traditions five-year retreats are customary. Let's start with a couple of hours.

If it is a short time, a couple of hours, you will probably be at home. Or you may have found you have some free time when away on holiday or a business trip. You do not have to fill in the empty space in the agenda: keep it empty. Go into the emptiness and you will emerge refreshed, more fulfilled. Set the time realistically. Put your answer-phone on. Turn the television or radio off. If you need to tell someone not to disturb you for the next couple of hours, do so. Put your work away or walk away from it. Then make a space.

The early Christian monks who lived much in solitude each had a cell. A monastic cell is different from a prison cell: you choose to be there. It is a place of stability, of security, of focus. It does not have to be elaborate. Cells are simple places. A chair, a cushion on the floor, a corner of a room. Make it tidy and clean. Set up a symbol of the presence; this could be a candle – ancient symbol of the presence of Christ – a flower, an icon, a photo, a cross, a Bible, or a simple everyday object. There should be a sense of simplicity, not clutter – of beauty, not prettiness. Have a watch or clock with a timer device nearby (not a loud ticker or too prominently placed).

With steadiness and ease: your body

Your retreat is a homecoming, an integrating, a remembering. It is not a spacewalk or a mind trip. You cannot come home unless you come inside, so take time to consider that you are also taking time to *make friends with your body*. And remember that you are only singling out the body for the purpose of the retreat. In fact you are really one single-woven tapestry of body–mind soaked and grounded in spirit: one being, fully alive.

[10]

Single out the body, then, and learn that it is happy to carry you, support you, hug you. It rejoices to pump blood, breathe, digest, walk, and sleep. It is a wonderful, mystical, funny contraption in which we are incarnated, and have epiphanies and transfigurations, and are crucified and resurrected.

Whatever you do on this retreat, keep breathing. Breathe as you take breakfast, as you go for a solitary walk or do some housework in your cell. Breathe while you are on the toilet. Breathe during your spiritual reading and as you doze off to a peaceful sleep after your day of silence.

You already have the three things necessary with which to make friends with your body. They are breath, gravity, and ground. You have been breathing since you were born and you will keep doing so as long as you need to. So relax and let breath breathe you. It is closer to you than your thinking. The way you breathe determines how you feel (see how your breathing changes when you are angry, frightened, or peaceful). As you give your attention to your breath you become naturally heavy. That is gravity hugging you. Give to it. Let it take you to the ground which stands under you (*understands you*). The ground comes up to hold you, so relax and do nothing. In fact, un-do. Let it. You just pay attention to the breath as it breathes you in and out, in and out.

You might enjoy lying on your back before and/or after your meditation times, or after a walk. Lying on your back is an excellent way to start making friends with your body on this retreat. It helps turn off all the tapes playing in your head: tapes telling you to make a good impression on others, to be demure or macho, how to look sexy or respectable, how to dominate and be noticed. When you lie down, the three bony boxes of your body – the head, chest, and pelvis – stop chattering to each other for a while and relate directly to the ground instead. It is like turning gravity off for a moment.

Lie on your back with your knees bent so that your lower back is quite flat on the floor. Let your chin drop lightly towards your chest so that it is no longer pointing up to the ceiling. If this is difficult, put a folded blanket under your head, just an inch or so, no more. And stay, and wait in silence or listen to a taped talk on meditation or some music. If you doze off, so be it. When you do get up, first roll over gently on to your hands and knees. It is not helpful to yank the head straightaway in order to get up, because that immediately undoes all the work that breath, gravity, and ground have just accomplished in straightening you out and un-knotting you.

If you want to take this friendship with your body further, you could read *Awakening the Spine* by Vanda Scaravelli, *Yoga Over 50* by Mary Stewart (even if you are 25), and *Yoga and You* by Esther Myers. These three women are yoga teachers of great depth, humour, and insight.

Lectio: your mind and its emotions
Then, sitting comfortably, read a section of this book. Read slowly. The book will last a long time, longer probably than your body. So there is no need to speed-read or devour the book and get on to another one. Re-read what you have read. Let your mind settle on a part of the passage which speaks to you most deeply. This may be just a phrase, a word, an image, or an idea. Revolve around that for a while. You don't have to analyse it. Savour it. The early desert monks called this *lectio*, spiritual (rather than mental) reading.

After a period of *lectio*, which can be ten or fifteen minutes, transfer your attention to the symbol which is the focal point for your retreat-space. Let your attention move towards the symbol, into the presence in the symbol. Let thought relax and the mind be still. When thoughts, fantasies, fears, anxieties, restlessness surface, let them come and let them go. Say, 'I'm sorry, you'll have to come and see me later. I'm busy doing nothing at the moment.' They will get the message if you give it strongly; be ruthless with them and don't compromise.

[12]

Meditation: going deeper

This would be a good time now for your meditation. Depending on how long you have been meditating or if you are just beginning, decide how many periods of meditation you are going to have during your retreat. A minimum would be two a day. Don't overdo it, but if you are a regular meditator you can profitably put additional periods in. More is not automatically better, of course. Three would be moderate. Six periods would be fine if you were sure you were not straining yourself or getting greedy.

Sit down with your back straight, sit still, close your eyes. Take a few deep breaths and then breathe normally. Then, silently, begin to repeat your word, your mantra. A good Christian mantra is the word *maranatha*. It means, 'Come, Lord,' or, 'The Lord comes,' but do not think of its meaning as you say it. Say the word simply and listen to it as you say it. This is the journey of faith, the deep listening. Faith leads to love. You could also take the word *Jesus* or *abba* (an Aramaic word used by Jesus, meaning 'father'). Whatever word you choose, stay with the same word throughout the meditation (and from one meditation period to the next) so that it can progressively take you deeper, from mind to heart.

Do not say the word with force. You are not trying to blank out the mind. Do not fight the thoughts which will come to you from every direction. Keep returning to the mantra. Say the word from the beginning to the end of the meditation whether you are aware of feeling distracted or peaceful. As soon as you realize you have stopped saying the word, start saying it again. In time (anywhere between five minutes and twenty years) the mantra will lead you at moments into complete stillness and silence, beyond itself. But if you are conscious of being silent then you are not yet completely silent, so keep on saying the mantra until the Spirit takes over. You will find that you say the mantra more deeply, more finely, more delicately as time goes on. Time your meditation with a timer – not too alarming a sound. If you are new to meditation, begin with twenty minutes (or less if you really find twenty too long). Other-

[13]

wise thirty minutes is a good period to meditate for. If you have a gong, this will help lead into and out of the meditation peacefully.

After the meditation, come out slowly. Open your eyes. Pay attention to the symbol you have set up in front of you. This would be a good time to read some scripture. *The Burning Heart* would be a good book to use at this point – a collection of John Main's favourite Scripture passages with a short commentary by him. Again, read slowly, chewing and savouring the Word. Don't gulp it down. You could then listen to some music, do some yoga, draw, or paint.

Structuring your time of retreat

If you have to get back to work and daily life, take a few moments to appreciate the gift of present you have just enjoyed – let it go, be non-possessive. Read another section of this book, again slowly and savouring what appeals to you. Open yourself to the next thing you have to do and prepare to do it while keeping your mind and heart open to the presence you have just turned towards. Your prayerfulness continues into whatever you are now going to do. And you can share the fruits of peace and joy you have received with others, not by preaching, but in the way you relate to them. If you need to, pack up your retreat things reverently and get on with life.

If you have more time you can vary the elements of this retreat time. If you have a whole day, for example, you could schedule two, three, or four meditations. This will depend somewhat on your experience in meditation. Don't overdo it, and more does not mean better. If you are making the retreat with others, that will introduce another dimension of presence. Use this book together, reading it aloud. If you have a weekend or even longer you will need to schedule your time more carefully. Draw up a timetable but allow yourself to be flexible in keeping to it. Morning, midday, and evening are natural times for prayer – and before you go to bed. If you have a day or longer on retreat, do some manual work, even housecleaning, and get some exercise and fresh air. Walk in

[14]

the garden or a park. Take this book with you and stop and read a section during your walk.

Don't just do something, sit there!
You might find the voice of conscience attacking you during your retreat. 'You are wasting your time,' it will say, or, 'You are being selfish.' You will think of all the practical, urgent, problematic things you could do. You will get an insight into a situation and want to dash off to implement it. Watch these restless thoughts and they will die down and return less frequently. This is why you will benefit from scheduling your time. It will fool your bush mind into thinking you are doing something productive. But your heart will teach you that you are not trying to produce or achieve anything. You are being. You are drinking deep, in the desert of modern life, of the waters of divine being. Your work and the people you live with, will all benefit from this time of retreat, so you are not being selfish. A gentle discipline in ordering your time of retreat – whether an hour or a day or a weekend – will help awaken a sense of inner freedom from anxiety, obsession, and fear. Enjoy it: find joy in it.

Laurence Freeman

Awakening

John Main

Conversion

But to this very day, every time the Law of Moses is read,
a veil lies over the minds of the hearers. However, as
Scripture says of Moses, 'whenever he turns to the Lord the
veil is removed'. Now the Lord of whom this passage
speaks is the Spirit; and where the Spirit of the Lord is,
there is liberty. And because for us there is no veil over the
face, we will reflect as in a mirror the splendour of the Lord;
thus we are transfigured into his likeness, from splendour
to splendour; such is the influence of the Lord who is
Spirit. (2 Cor. 3:15-18)

'Whenever he turns to the Lord the veil is removed.'

I want to begin our retreat with a reflection on the meaning of
conversion. The principal vow that St Benedict had his monks
take was the vow of conversion. And for St Benedict this Latin
word means 'to turn wholly towards'. It is a complete turning towards which is the beginning of our experience of the kingdom of
God. For St Benedict, being converted marks the beginning of our
experience of God's kingdom at work within us.

Now we know that if we turn towards something, this implies
that we turn away from something else. So if we are going to be
converted, if we are going to turn towards the Lord, we are going
to have, as it were, to change our field of vision. What we need to
do is recover the sense that our conversion is a continuing process.
It is not as though we were converted once for all time. Our conversion, in other words, is never complete. If we can once understand 'conversion' then there is an end to complacency, an end to

resting on our oars. To really understand conversion we have to be on the move and on the way.

Benedictines have produced a vast scholarship on the Rule of St Benedict, and one big question often arises. Did St Benedict use the word *conversio* or did he use the word *conversatio*? That might seem like a bit of rather petty scholarship – did a scribe just miss out two letters when he was copying the Rule? – but it is a very, very important question because the Latin word *conversio* means an act of change or a group of acts of change which can be suggested by the outward signs of our lives. But the other word, *conversatio*, is more than just the outward sign. The word *conversatio* is much more about the continuous spirit of conversion which creates in us an awareness that turning towards God is a dynamic process, not something that we have accomplished once and for all. *Conversatio* is a dynamic process, an ongoing process, a 'turning toward the Lord', in the words of St Paul, so that we can gaze more fully upon his face and in gazing upon his face 'we are transfigured into his likeness from splendour to splendour'.

What I hope to suggest to you is that there are two levels of conversion. There is the outward level of the external aspects of our lives. But underneath this level of exterior conversion is an internal conversion, what you might call a conversion of heart. And if we are simply living at the external level without the deeper, inner conversion of heart then we are in danger of our spiritual life being merely outward, dry, formal, and legalistic. Where you are in your exterior life ultimately depends on what is going on at the deeper level. Namely: What is going on in your heart? The term for conversion that St Benedict preferred, following St Paul, was *conversatio*, namely the deeper level of your heart being really open to the wonder and to the mystery of God.

I want to suggest to you that the conversion that we are talking about here is a continuous and continuously deepening commitment to that fundamental level of our spirit which is constantly responding to the spirit Christ has placed in our hearts. St Paul suggests this in his letter to the Philippians. 'For our conversation', he says, 'is in heaven; from whence also we look for the Saviour, the Lord Jesus Christ' (Phil. 3:20, AV). In modern English, the meaning of that text is not so self-evident. I often used to wonder when I was a child, 'What on earth does this mean – "our conversation is in heaven"?' I thought there must a lot of chatter going on there. But in fact, of course, St Paul is talking about the deep levels of conversion – *conversatio*. What he is saying, in effect, is, 'Let your heart be turned toward the Lord.'

I want to spend a little time just looking at this concept of *conversio* which is so central to the Christian revelation as it appears in the Bible; and I also want to spend time looking at the Old Testament.

Repentance, in the Old Testament, is the experience of our need to be converted. I think it is no exaggeration to say that this is the central experience of the Jewish people. It is perhaps the main experience which distinguished the Jewish people from the pagans among whom they lived, the idol worshippers. If we can turn to God and open ourselves to his power, then his power to transform and to transfigure us is absolutely limitless. This was the truth analysed and proclaimed by the prophets. Even before the prophets there was this sense of turning away from self, and turning to the Lord. There were outward signs of sin: the sackcloth, the ashes, the rending of garments, the formulas of lamentation. All of that existed in the Jewish law and they were the outward signs of this inward turning towards the Lord. Yet despite all this elaborate ritual, all this elaborate external conversion, the prophets increasingly called for what they called real conversion. Amos, for example, called not just for outward worship but for a changed heart, a changed conduct in the service of justice. Hosea called for a turning away from idolatry and a turning towards real knowledge of God.

Let us humble ourselves, let us strive to know the LORD;
whose justice dawns like the morning light ...
Loyalty is my desire, not sacrifice,
not whole-offerings but the knowledge of God.

(Hosea 6: 3,6)

The Jewish experience of the importance of conversion is the common religious experience of practically all peoples. But we can so easily diffuse the power of God. We can make our religion just the fulfilling of external rites, sacrifices, rules and so forth where the heart, the knowledge of God, is asleep. And when you come to consider it, what can be a greater shattering of our own complacency than the knowledge of God? If we could really know who God is, if we could really have that experience of the reality of his presence, then our own lack of religious commitment is exposed and we are utterly shattered. Turning to the Lord – the knowledge of God – brings with it a profound silence. Once we have encountered the Spirit of the living God, the only authentic response possible is a profound and reverential silence.

The thing we have to face with the challenge of conversion is that we do have to be changed. We like to think that we are going to change ourselves in our own time and at our own pace. But the essence of conversion is that in turning to the Lord he changes us. I suppose the reality with most of us is that we are not too keen on being changed. We much prefer to run the show at our own pace. We like to call the shots and have things under our control. The essence of conversion is that the Lord God is going to call the shots, and we are going to be changed as he wants us to be changed. As you continue to say the mantra, and as you deepen your silence in prayer, do not be surprised if you find in yourself some strong reservations about it, even some annoyance about it, possibly some anger about it. What dawns on us as we experience more fully the poverty of it, is that it is now quite literally the Lord's prayer, not mine any longer. We have given up our own

[22]

words; we have given up our own monologues; we have given up our own recitations. Now it is the Lord's prayer because we respond at his pleasure. Once that begins to dawn on us, we can get quite restless because most of us, if we are honest, do not really want to be changed. We want to have our religion under our control just in the same way that we want to have most other things and most other people under our own control.

This tendency was clear to the Jewish prophets. Jeremiah, the great prophet of repentance, declared that repentants must not be content merely to weep and confess their sins but they must change their conduct and cleave their hearts wide open to the Lord. We all have to face our lack of sincerity, our lack of honesty, our lack of integrity.

As we read that passage from Jeremiah we might begin to think of Dame Julian of Norwich. She used that wonderful expression that 'God himself is the ground of our beseeching.' But this basic Christian insight is not cosy. It releases the shattering power of love into our life. John Donne prayed for this violence of love in one of his poems: 'Batter my heart, three person'd God'. Unless we have this divine violence applied to us, we will not undergo a fundamental conversion of heart in the ground of our beseeching.

The Greek Bible uses two words for what we translate into English as 'repentance'. The first, *epistrephein*, refers to the outward sign of conversion, and the second, *metanoia*, refers to the real inner conversion of heart. These are synonyms of the two words that highlight St Benedict's conversion: *conversio* and *conversatio*.

What I want to stress for you is that all the outward signs of our life – our religious observances, our prayer and fasting, our new resolutions to live better – are all good things, but all of these mean nothing, or very little, unless there is this inner conversion of heart, this inner poverty of spirit. This is the secret of the saying: 'Blessed are the poor in spirit.'

What the Old Testament prophets were talking about – what

this word *metanoia* means – is conversion of heart. Don't rend your garments but let your hearts be clean, open to the Lord. That is something that we must bear in mind and heart with absolute honesty. It is conversion of heart that counts. The outward signs are only effective signs if they really are signs of something that we experience inwardly, deeply in our hearts.

Jesus himself was heralded by the the the last of the Old Testament prophets, John the Baptist, who, as it were, summed up in himself the cry to repentance of all his predecessors. Jesus described his own vocation as coming to call sinners to repentance. He did so not by referring to the penitential practices of the synagogues but by a call to a change of heart. Now the change of heart that Jesus calls us to is that we become like little children. And that is a fundamental change of heart once we have lost our innocence.

When you think of it, this call is a really surprising climax to the sort of a high-pitched tone that the Old Testmant prophets had been engaged in. Becoming like little children sounds very simple and direct, and it is part of the extraordinary climax of the whole of the New Testament revelation. It is why Jesus' contemporaries found it so difficult. They were expecting this great Messiah who was going to sweep the board clean and defeat the Romans. What does John say? 'There is the Lamb of God' (John 1:36). They are all expecting a lion, and what do they get? A lamb. And what is his message? His message is not that you will become the great spiritual giants of the latter day, but that you will become as little children.

We have got to understand clearly that to his fellow Jews and to us this was a shocking climax to the whole of the Old Testament. It was a shocking anti-climax and it can be equally shocking to us. What Jesus is calling us to is simplicity. He is calling us away from the error of giving primary importance to external signs and manifestations. He does so by his loving reassurance to us that we are the beloved sons and daughters of God, sending his Spirit into our hearts. And that is the Spirit of gentleness, compassion and love.

I want to stress that concept of repentance as simplicity because we have got so hooked in to the complex language of contemporary psychology. We have to consider, quite rightly, questions like self-fulfilment. How will a person today come to full maturity? We all use those words and ideas and they are right for us to pursue, but the way we come to Christian fulfilment and maturity, is by listening to the Lord Jesus as our teacher. His words to us are, 'Unless you turn round and become like children you will never enter the kingdom of heaven' (Matt. 18:3). That is the task that we have and the message that we carry to others. It is a very difficult one in a world that worships complexity and which has lost its innocence.

What is a little child? What on earth is it that Jesus is talking about here? As far as I can see, what he is talking about is the wholeness of the child, the innocence of the child. The childlike quality that comes through to us in Jesus' teaching is the sort of fearless integrity and freedom a child has. A child likes to look at you. He or she will come up, throw their arms round your neck and give you a big hug and a kiss. They are not terrified that you are going to reject them. The child is not terrified that he is going to make a fool of himself. There is a wholeness and an integrity there which as adults we must reclaim at higher levels of our development. William James, in his essay on the nature of religious experience, speaks of this innocence as being 'the healing of the wound of the divided self'. That is what ongoing conversion leads us to. It puts one very much in mind of the Russian mystics who talk about the central task of prayer being to bring heart and mind back into their original unity.

I think that what we have got to get clearly into our heads is that our call to conversion is a call to turn to Christ, to gaze upon him, to listen to him. The qualities that we need are attention, patience to wait on the Lord, and simplicity. William James puts this very well when he says, 'The real witness of the spirit to the second birth is to be found only in the disposition of the genuine child of

God, the permanently patient heart, the love of self eradicated.'
And he quotes Martin Luther: 'The foolishness of man's heart is
so great that he rather seeketh to himself more laws to satisfy his
conscience ... But here, except thou do quite the contrary, except
thou send Moses away with his law, and in these terrors and this
anguish lay hold upon Christ who died for thy sins, look for no
salvation' (*The Varieties of Religious Experience* Longmans, 1902;
Penguin, 1982, p. 245). As you know there was quite a strong move
at the Vatican Council to canonize Martin Luther, but it failed. It
was a very awkward situation! The more one reads of Luther, the
more one can see what profound religious insights he has. One
wonders what was going on at the Vatican in his time! But what
about Luther's idea of the church? He had an exceptional insight
that was central, that the church was not primarily about the en-
forcement of rules but about holding to Christ. Faith for Christians
is to lay hold upon Christ, which is, as St Paul says, to grasp God's
secret. And that secret is Christ.

William James calls conversion the state of assurance. It is a
state of assurance simply because we have laid hold upon Christ.
We are turned towards him. We are rooted in him, founded in him,
and grounded in him. These are the signs Jesus gives of the person
who is really converted: First of all assurance, loss of worry and a
sense that all in life is ultimately meaningful. Secondly, a growing
lucidity, the mystery of life becoming clearer. Thirdly, a new sense
of duty. Every object becomes beautified by God's providence.
And lastly, an ecstasy of happiness. Those are the fruits of conversion. Now that is our invitation: to turn to the Lord, and in turning
to him to be transformed and transfigured.

Questions for Reflection:
1. In my own life am I able to discern a process of continual conversion? How have I facilitated that process? How have I hindered
it?

[26]

2. 'Let your heart be turned toward the Lord.'
Do I see that statement as a realistic or an idealistic goal? In my daily life, how do I respond to that exhortation?

3. What place does silence hold in my spiritual journey? How can I develop a deeper appreciation and love of silence?

4. How do I respond to the call of Jesus to become like a little child? What concrete steps do I take in my life to become like a little child?

Application:
How can I adjust my daily activities and practices so that I can nurture the process of conversion and develop a taste for deeper silence?

> What we must do is to begin to meditate, to begin to open ourselves up to the love of God and its power. To do this, all we need to do is to begin to say the mantra, lovingly and in a deep spirit of faith. (*Word Into Silence*, p. 17)

Meditate for thirty minutes.

Leadership

Let us examine the leadership that we need to respect and practise in order to turn towards Christ at every level of our lives – wholehearted conversion.

The leader appears in every society as some kind of social being, but there are different sorts of leaders. There is a difference, for example, between a leader like Alexander the Great in Ancient Greece and a modern American president. Or there is a difference between a religious leader like St Benedict and some modern emotive evangelical preacher. I want to put before you a distinction between two great types of leader. The first I would identify as the hero and the second as the father figure. I would see Alexander the Great and St Benedict as heroic figures, or heroes. I would see most of the modern presidents and most of the evangelical preachers of today as father figures. The distinction is not based on the ideas or the methods the leader uses, but much more on the scope of his vision; his vision of human nature, his vision of his own age. Above all the hero is distinguished from the father figure by the long-term consequences of his life among us. Heroes are for ever, fathers for their generation.

The hero, according to Carl Jung, is an archetype that we find expressed in many myths and fairy tales. The hero leaves his family, leaves his friends and embarks upon an adventure. In the great fairy tales or folk tales or myths of most societies, this adventure will be either the slaying of a monster or the freeing of some innocent victim of evil or the discovery of his origins. When the hero has succeeded in his mission he is rewarded with a happy marriage and fulfilment. Most of us might like to think that the tale should end there and indeed in our modern cinema and television fantasies that are constructed around this archetype, this is indeed where the show usually does end so that they all live happily ever after. This probably leaves most of us with a sense of incompletion. What did they do next? How did it actually work out?

Jung points out that the full expression of the symbol is when the hero is himself sacrificed or killed like Siegfried or the Egyptian Osiris. Then, in the fullest symbolism, the hero rises from the dead. But rather than returning to earth as before, he reigns in a kingdom that is not of this world.

Antony Storr, a psychologist writing on Jung, says of this great archetypal heroic story that the death of the hero could be taken as signifying the turning point in life, the turning point at which the ego has to relinquish the seat of power, when it has to acknowledge a dependence upon something or someone greater than itself. That is it is essential for us to understand the life, death, and resurrection of Jesus.

The hero, in his life and as often in his death, leads because he stimulates his fellow men and women by his magnanimous vision, generosity of heart and, above all, by his example of courage. The hero opens horizons and develops creativity among his followers. His call is a call to share in the adventure that he has discovered himself, perhaps at the cost of his life. It is an adventure that is not without its dangers, but not without its rewards either. The essence of the adventure to which this hero summons us is that it is not an adventure that we simply undertake by our own choice, but an adventure to which we are *called*: a vocation.

The father figure is sometimes misinterpreted by his devotees as a hero, despite the fact that real heroes do not encourage hero-worship. The father figure is above all a protecting figure. The father figure protects where the hero explores, takes risks. The father figure does the thinking for the society; his principal concern is to show those he leads safe. The father figure 'knows it all', whereas the hero says to his followers, 'The adventure is beginning. We have more to find out.' And that expansion of our consciousness – if we continue the quest with courage – is infinite.

'The adventure is beginning.' This is what we must understand. It is what we were talking about earlier. We can never in life achieve a perfect, protected situation. We are always responding more and more generously, more and more magnanimously to the vision that unfolds before us. A very interesting example is the story of an anthropologist who was working in Kenya in the 1940s. While he was investigating a particular tribe he was amazed to hear that the members of that tribe had no dreams. Later he realized that what they were saying to him was that they attached no significance to their dreams. Even the simple fact that they attached no significance to their dreams seemed to him to be rather strange and he found out that it was the medicine men who did the dreaming for the tribe because it was the medicine men's role to foretell the future and to interpret the social symbols. But when he approached the medicine men he discovered that they too had stopped dreaming. He asked them, 'How long have you stopped dreaming?' And he was told they had stopped dreaming when the British district officer arrived. In other words, the white man, the colonial administrator, had become the tribe's father figure in place of the medicine man because it was the white man who made their decisions, shaped their future and protected them.

Now we should be very wary, too, of thinking of the heroic leader merely as a mythic or primitive phenomenon. The heroic leader is, in fact, called forth by the developed consciousness, not by the undeveloped consciousness. The heroic leader appears in ancient Greece, a highly developed and sophisticated society. A desperate and broken Germany produced the father figure of Hitler. That was why Nazi Germany became a barbarian society. It is the primitive not the civilized society which, being hide-bound by fear, seeks the comforting protection of the father figure.

St Benedict, as I understand his role, is a heroic leader, a man called forth by a civilized and developed society. His leadership is incarnated in his Rule, which is a rule of life written for those who have chosen an adventure. The spiritual life is this quest to find yourself, to find God, to find your fellow human beings. It is the greatest adventure there is.

The Rule of St Benedict is by no means a manifesto. The first word in the Rule is 'Listen.' That is the theme of the entire Rule: 'Listen.' And the last word in the Rule is that if you persevere you will get there. Now this seems perhaps rather a modest statement of Benedict's role as a leader, but I think modesty is the way. Most people of genius have been aware that their work will live after them even if they are denied recognition in their own lifetime and therefore many of them write with an eye on posterity. But the Rule of St Benedict shows a complete concentration on the present. This is what makes it timeless. It has a note of true, realistic humility, and that is what has made it last. For five centuries practically every important figure on the world stage was brought up under the direct influence of the Rule of St Benedict. For five centuries the Rule was the best known text apart from the Bible. It was the early inspiration of most of the founders of modern Europe, scholars and politicians alike: Augustine, Anselm, Lanfranc, Gregory the Great, Gregory VII, Boniface and Bede.

Now St Benedict the man and the Rule of St Benedict are one and the same entity for us if only because we know so little about his life that is not legend, and we know so little of him that is not conveyed through the Rule. But St Gregory, who wrote St Benedict's life, gives us one very clear insight into his character. Benedict could not abide the Roman schools of his day and he fled them. Gregory said of him that he was 'deliberately ignorant and wisely uneducated'. Like many another man of genius before and since, Benedict was able to transcend the cultural concepts of his own time because he had never been brainwashed. His spirit had never been broken by an 'excellent education'. Of any harm that I may have done as an 'educator', one of the things that has always struck me as the most terrible is that children come to school with a real creative mind, with real fresh ways of looking at things, and what we so readily do is to brainwash them to give them the received opinions, so they will be able to hand back those received opinions and get good grades. We then say that this child is very well educated. That is the great tragedy of so much modern education, its lack of heroic leadership preparing children for the adventure of life.

As I said, we know St Benedict through the Rule and the Rule shows us Benedict above all as a man of authority. I would like to make a distinction here. The hallmark of the father figure or the mother figure is authoritarianism. The hallmark of the heroic leader is authority. As we know from the Gospels, it was widely felt that Christ was a man of authority, and the Pharisees and the council of the Sanhedrin were authoritarians. In listening to Benedict we do not find brilliant epigrams. We detect authoritative force because every part of the Rule points to the same centre. It is this inner coherence that explains the Rule's authority and longevity. Other works have achieved this reality too, but they have not had so powerful an influence because they lack what seems to me to epitomize the achievement of the Rule – what we might call its modesty and realistic compassion.

St Benedict clearly appears as a human being with a very great human heart. His authority is in proportion to his confidence in his own judgement. He says, 'Listen, my son, to the commands of your master.' This natural self- assurance of the really heroic leader is not tied to any static or egotistic view of self. He says, 'Let all follow the Rule as master.' In other words, he shows that the man and his message are absolutely identified. Benedict the man flows out of his own being, the narrow confines of the self, into the universal relevance of the Rule. This is what makes him speak with authority as the *author*.

We all know that if we are to be inspired to undertake a dangerous journey, if we are going to extend the frontiers of our own knowledge, we will need a leader with confidence and vision

who will state his/her wisdom and his/her experience clearly
and with authority. The voice of the Rule, I think, is the voice of
the free man. St Benedict comes through as a man who has
gained his freedom by his transcendence of self. He really has
escaped from the narrow, confining limits of his own ego.
Nowhere is freedom so excitingly proclaimed as in Benedict's
vision of community.

Remember that St Benedict, writing in the sixth century, pro-
vides this workable process for a fully democratic participatory
process of government: 'Often when very important business has
to be done in the monastery let the abbot call together the whole
community and himself set the matter before them. Now the reason why we have said that all should be called to council is that
God often reveals what is better to the younger.' Now that is a most
extraordinary statement to come out of the sixth century and I am
sorry to say that it has been obeyed more in the breach than in ob-
servance down through the intervening fourteen centuries, because so many of us older folks are so consistently convinced that
our experience helps us to know everything better than the young.
What does T.S. Eliot say?

> There is, it seems to us,
> At best, only a limited value
> In the knowledge derived from experience.
> The knowledge imposes a pattern, and falsifies.
> ... Do not let me hear
> Of the wisdom of old men, but rather of their folly,
> Their fear or fear and frenzy, their fear of possession,
> Of belonging to another, or to others, or to God.
> The only wisdom we can hope to acquire
> Is the wisdom of humility: humility is endless.
>
> (*Four Quartets*)

That is what St Benedict was trying to put before us. The heroic
leader has no need to fear this community wisdom. He will not be

threatened if one of the younger brethren comes out with an idea that he had never thought of himself.

Freedom to share life this way with one another can only be achieved by one who has transcended the self-protecting, anxious fears of the unrenewed ego. St Benedict was only able to proclaim this participatory community view of religious life because he was a man who had a full Christian confidence in himself and a basic trust in human nature. This is not necessarily or essentially a confidence in his own personal talents or gifts. It is the confidence of a man who has achieved the liberty to love others with total self-transcendence. In other words, St Benedict's authority is born of his loving kindness, of his concern for others, his selflessness, his extraordinary generosity and largeness of heart. When you read the Rule you will find that he has special words for the care and patience necessary for community life. You see it in his caring for the very young. There is a care and delicacy also when dealing with the very old, the sick, and even more wonderfully with the ignorant or the timid, and very, very humanly for the slow-moving. If ever you have walked down a cloister behind some old monk shuffling along as you are trying to get somewhere in a hurry you realize the wonderful sensitivity of St Benedict. *Slowly.* Imagine the heart of the man that he even put that view in his Rule and expressed concern for the timid, too. It shows his extraordinary sensitivity towards every type of person.

The life of his community has this threefold element: *oratio, lectio,* and *labor.* The purpose of this division is to emphasize the wholeness of the life of prayer and discipline which constitutes the monastic adventure. The purpose of the spiritual life, in his vision, is to lead each one of us to full humanity, the fullest possible development of all our potentialities. The monastery, as a community, is a community that is always growing into a deeper, deepening Christian vitality. The monastery is a place where there is *life,* life in Christ. The Rule was the great turning point in the development of monastic life because it laid down reasonable

[34]

and realistic foundations for the discovery of the source of life. It laid down a flexible framework of our search for God. Within this framework there would be wise teachers who have made the journey ahead of the beginners who are still on the pilgrimage but want, like their leaders, to make progress.

The essence of the elders in the community of St Benedict is that they shall be inspirational for the younger members. Their courage, their sensitivity and their humanity will inspire the beginners in achieving their own particular path of development. Again and again in the Rule therefore we are reminded of the dangers of losing touch with reality. For Benedict, reality is the great touchstone of contemplative living. We must always be on guard against becoming eccentric or isolated. Again and again, the value by which life is shaped is shown to be fellowship in community, mutual love. 'Let them love one another', he says, 'with a chaste love.' Our first goal in life is to be more firmly grasped by reality and always to beware of losing touch with it.

But again Benedict is a mature man and a realist. He is constantly aware, as T. S. Eliot was, that 'human kind cannot bear very much reality'. The true seeker, in Benedict's vision, is the person who is constantly increasing his or her capacity to bear more and more reality and to share it with others in the loving spirit of community. The wisdom-path of St Benedict is therefore also the way of gentleness and compassion.

Questions for Reflection:
1. Who are the people I identify as heroes? What heroic qualities do/did they exhibit? Is there evidence in my life that I try to emulate these heroes in some way?

2. Who do I identify as father/mother figures? What loving qualities do/did they exhibit?

[35]

3. St Benedict's Rule begins with the word 'Listen'. To whom or to what do I listen? What do I hear?

4. There is only one wisdom and that is the wisdom of humility.' What do I see as the difference between knowledge and wisdom? Would I rather know a lot, or be wise?

Application:
I will listen more attentively to the word of God by making time each day for spiritual reading. I will read a passage from Scripture and let it enter my heart. I will carry the word of Scripture with me throughout the day.

> When we look at the New Testament, at least when we look at it with eyes enlightened by the spirit of Christ burning in our hearts, we cannot but become intoxicated, amazed at the sheer wonder of the destiny that is given to each of us. But, we must always remember that the condition of being open to this, and of responding to our destiny, is always simplicity, poverty of spirit. It means we are invited by the same destiny to leave behind all complexity, all desire to possess God or to possess spiritual knowledge and to tread the narrow way of dispossession. We require faithfulness. We learn to be faithful by being simply faithful to the daily times of meditation and, during the meditation, to the saying of the mantra. (*The Way of Unknowing*, p. 3)

Meditate for thirty minutes.

The church - a community of love

I want to say something about the church. It is very important that we should find out exactly where we are in our relationship with the church. First of all if you ask yourself the question, 'What is the church?' you are almost bound to come up with an idea that the church is something outside us, an entity or institution that is external to us. I think that when we begin to think about the church we have to ask ourselves not so much 'What is the church?' but 'Who am I?' or, better still, 'Who are we?' I think if we ask ourselves this question, the answer we arrive at concerning the church will not be a sterile, juridical one, speaking in terms of official membership, institution, hierarchy, and so forth. But we will begin to see that the church is itself a living creature that has come into being through the redemptive activity of Christ. And it is kept alive by a double pulse. First there is the pulse of the love of God that he extends continually toward us - what St Paul called the Spirit pleading for us (Romans 8:26). The second pulse is the pulse of our willing and wholehearted acceptance of that love. In other words, allowing our hearts to beat in unison with his. And because our hearts beat in unison with his, they beat in unity, one with another. This is the way in which we allow his love to enter us, and what inspires us to bring that love to the world. So I think what we have got to see is, in the language of Scripture, that we are the living stones that make up the church. We ourselves are new creatures born in this newness of life because we have entered into this new fellowship, this new relationship with God, and with one another.

A lot of people have reservations about this theology, because they see it as being excessively optimistic. They think there is a danger that we could become intoxicated by the optimistic freedom of thoughts like this. But I do not think any of us need to be reminded that if we have been born again in Christ, we do have this new relationship to one another and this relationship creates the church. None of us, I think, needs to be reminded either that there is a certain dead, pessimistic weight in us that rebels against this daily transformation: the transformation that requires a continuous conversion to the person of Christ. And that ongoing turning is what makes a person more deeply Christian. What makes a person more effectively and more fully a member of the church is this constant deepening of one's conversion. That is a very different thing from just amassing increasing information about Christ or his church or just being 'obedient'.

I suggest to you that the reason we have to ask the question, 'Who am I?' or 'Who are we,' is because if we do not open our deep selves to Christ and allow our whole lives to be transformed in Christ, we have at best only a very limited opportunity to find out who we really are. It seems to me that the church is above all a community in which a person has a new power to know and a new power to love. The invitation to join the church is an invitation to deeper, less isolated individuality, to deeper, more altruistic personal growth, and to deeper fulfilment. Each of us has a deeper power to know through faith, and a deeper power to love through charity. By entering the church's community of faith and love we know that we are known and that we are loved.

If we speak of the church in terms of a particular Christian church, such as the Roman Catholic church, we must also have a complementary understanding of our own local church. Every spiritual community is in itself in some sense a microcosm of the church. I think we must all be very clear that the invitation to be a member of a faith community is an invitation to achieve one's own deepest, personal fulfilment, to become most perfectly the person one is called to be. We recognize that we will come to be the person we are called to be by being rooted in Christ, the one who is himself most deeply personal, and who reveals to us the fullness of the personhood of God. What we have to witness to is that in the church, in our communities, the individual can never live merely as an individual. We are bound to express what we are: one bound in love to others, in a love that is outward-looking and redeemed. The church, then, is not so much something outside us which we enter; it is rather the church that enters us, or emerges from deep within us. At baptism the bond of love unites us to Christ and to our fellow Christians. Christ enters us. It is only in this sense that we are born 'into' the church.

I want to reflect for a moment upon some of the Biblical images of the church to see if we can deepen our understanding of it by using the imagination of the Jewish people. One of the favourite descriptions of the church is that it is a temple constructed of living stones. That is a marvellous image of the church – that each of us has an integral function in it. Each of us is absolutely essential, whether as a little slate up on the roof keeping the rains off or as a great big foundation stone down below not seen above the surface but keeping the whole thing up. Or we may be like those people that all communities have, a kind of flying buttress on the outside. Whatever our function, we have an integral, essential role in the whole structure, and the whole structure is giving glory to God. So the idea of the temple is a magnificent and compelling image; but it does have the great disadvantage of being a static concept. And whether you are a flying buttress or a great foundation stone down below, you are just there – plonk! – and that is it. But our experience of being the church is something far more dynamic.

Another concept of the church which St Paul likes is as the living body with Christ as its head. For St John it is a living vine with the branches rooted in the true vine. It is a city with its origin in heaven. In these living examples of the vine and the body, I think we have the best images of the church. It is something that is constantly growing, developing and changing, but always drawing strength and direction from the true vine, from the head of the body, the Lord Jesus. Its root is deep in the ground of being.

An image of the church that I like very much myself is that of a bride constantly preparing to meet her spouse who is God. I was at home for the weddings of my three sisters, and each time the whole house was thrown into complete chaos because of the well-known vanity of my family. My sisters were always dashing back to take a last look in the mirror to see that their veil was exactly at the right angle or whatever it was, preparing to stagger everyone in the church with their astonishing beauty. The image of the bride constantly preparing to meet her spouse has a really dynamic element to it. We are always open to the love of Jesus, always open and prepared to be, as it were, his loved one.

What I want to stress by these examples is that all of us must accept the responsibility to be constantly creating and recreating the church. That is an aspect of ecclesiology that we have not been so clear on in the past. The church is co-created by us. We have this responsibility. I can tell you a family story that illustrates how strongly some people love the church and how they feel 'responsible' for it.

I have very rarely in my life heard a sermon interrupted by a parishioner – except by my father who was a very wild Kerryman. For a while we lived in London and my father had a most beloved parish priest there who also came from Kerry. Everyone revered this man as a saint. But this priest was not very good at keeping financial accounts. In fact, he had a small parlour in the presbytery which he kept locked, and when the Sunday collections were taken in he just opened the door, threw what was in the plates into the room, and then locked the door again. When the milkman came to be paid, or whatever it was, the priest would go in on his hands and knees and scoop out the money that was required. When the priest died, having kept the accounts like this for twenty years or so, there was absolute chaos so that the archbishop sent the most efficient priest in the diocese to try and sort this whole thing out. He was a very nice, a somewhat correct and formal English man. My father was very, very disappointed when this poor fellow arrived after the death of the previous one. After he had been there a year, the English man got up to render an account of his stewardship and he announced that when he had arrived in the parish things were in a state of terrible chaos caused by the previous priest who had clearly been no financial manager. My father was getting rather upset. Then the new priest went on with his sermon from the pulpit denouncing his predecessor over and over again. To my mother's horror and to the utter horror of the entire congregation, the next thing you know my father jumped up saying, 'Will you get down from there!' Now my father was a fairly formidable fellow. He was about six foot three with a big mop of curly black hair. The priest was unwise enough to try to argue with my father, at which time my father began striding up the church saying, 'If you don't get down, I shall put you down!' The priest at that stage thought better of it and he moved nippily to the altar, closing the altar rail door as he got inside. My father, I think, had some idea that *he* also was responsible for the church and for the good name of the man he loved who had been the pastor. In his own rather eccentric way he decided that he would accept that responsibility.

I think all of us have to come to a much more living view of the church in that or a similar real way; that we accept our responsbility. We cannot just sit back criticizing the church or criticizing the bishops or the pope. We have our own responsbility to the church and in that sense we create it. There must be constant interaction between all members of the Body of Christ. Because it is *all* members of the Body of Christ that create it and that is what makes, or should make, the church such an extraordinarily rich, vital, enriching, and vitalizing society to belong to.

I think that we must recover the sense of the power of Christ at work in the church. For example, if you look at the letter to the Ephesians, you find very clearly in the theology of Paul that Christ has entered into our own death. Christ has liberated us from death, by being exalted at the right hand of the Father. What St Paul then shows us is that Christ here and now calls forth this liberating power in and through the church – not the church as some hierarchic, static institution, but the church that is the family of God, the household of God, the redeemed of God – the church as those who *know* that they are the redeemed of God and who know that they are part of his household. Listen to his words: 'You are no longer aliens or foreign visitors. You are citizens like all the saints and part of God's household. You are part of the building that has the apostles and the prophets for its foundation. And Christ Jesus is himself the main cornerstone. And as every structure is aligned upon him all grow into one holy temple in the Lord' (Eph. 2:19–21, author's translation). Then he adds, using the present tense of the verb, 'and you too, in him, are being built into a house where God lives in the Spirit' (Eph. 2:22, author's translation).

What is abundantly clear for St Paul is that the church is the continuation among humankind of what God effected in Christ. And this continuation of the Christ-life is achieved through the activity of the Spirit. The Spirit is, as it were, not sent merely into an institution; the Spirit is sent into the hearts of men and women, raising them to a state in which they themselves are the expression in this world of the Risen Christ. The mystery of the church is that this work of continuing among humankind what God effected in Christ is done with men and women not as mere individuals, but as a community. Listen again to Ephesians: 'For he (God) brought us back to life with Christ and he raises us up with him and he gives us a place with him in heaven in Christ Jesus' (Eph. 2:6–7, author's translation). In other words, for St Paul the church is constituted by those who recognize the living Christ in their midst, the living Spirit of Christ in their hearts.

All the images of the Bible have this in common, that the Christian has his or her meaning as a Christian because of belonging to this new community, this new family, this new fellowship.

It is the fellowship of those who recognize the Lord Jesus and his Spirit in their hearts and in the hearts of their fellow members of the church, the community. The church is not a community which destroys or smothers individuality. The church is a community in which we find our true individuality through community. It is especially in St John that we see this meaning of the church as the fellowship, though 'fellowship' is a very poor word in modern English. We do not have a good one-word translation of the Greek *koinonia* in modern English. For St John, the church is this friendly, warm-hearted, loyal, mutually caring fellowship which has come down from heaven in order to create among humankind a society that is an expression of the fellowship of the union that exists among the three persons of the most Holy Trinity itself. The Johannine vision is that the most perfect community is the most Holy Trinity, and that the church is composed of those who enter into this relationship in union with the most Holy Trinity. The church in this sense is the Word become flesh in order to serve the Father, and in order to enter into the total service of humankind.

For St John the church, as the Christ-presence in the world, is above all to be recognized by its dedication to the teaching of Jesus and by its service of others. For John, it is through the service of Jesus that this new fellowship is brought into being. It is a fellowship in his victimhood, in his service of us, and above all, a fellowship with his risen life. This centring of our lives on Christ in the Spirit to the Father is the central theme of John's priestly prayer of Christ: 'May they all be one, Father. May they be one in us as you are in me and I am in you, so that the world may believe that it was you who sent me' (John 17:21, author's translation). Here is a point that we have got to take very much to heart. Our unity in the church, and in our communities, is the touchstone of our effectiveness in proclaiming the gospel. For John it is our unity that is the great sign of the church as the presence in this world of the Father, of Jesus, and of the Holy Spirit.

[43]

Mistakes in the church down through history have smothered individuality and made the church into an authoritarian institution; most of those mistakes have been made because Christians have not seen the importance of this unity. But it is a unity that can never be brought about by force. It is a unity that cannot be brought about by merely organizational structures. It is not uniformity. It is a unity that has to be based above all in the reality of the Spirit which is apprehended in the hearts of the individual members of the church. And so the central idea in the Johannine theology is of union with Christ and of the union of Christ within the unity of the most Holy Trinity. For the early church, Christian worship was simply the way for men and women to enter most deeply into this union.

I would like to end for now by stressing that it is in the church, with that Spirit-dimension to it, that we find the possibility for the greatest fullness in our own lives. We have to be aware of that fullness and ensure that it is known as a real and present possibility.

Questions for Reflection:

1. Who am I? Who am I as a member of a church? Who am I as a member of a community of believers? Who are we together?

2. How do I sense the pulse of God's love in my heart? How do I respond to the church as institution or as fellowship?

3. How do I accept God's love?

4. The church is constructed from living stones. How do I bind myself to the other members of my faith community? How do I let them become united with me in Christ?

5. How do I show my responsibility to the well-being of the church community and of the church's relationship with the world?

Application:
I will open myself more fully to the inspiration of the Holy Spirit in my life. I will try to discern more clearly what gifts I might offer to the church community. I will also see how I can take responsibility for the way the church presents itself to the world.

> Our Christian communities do not exist for themselves, but for others and ultimately for the Other. In our prayer we have to discover ourselves existing for the Other because it is in prayer that we experience ourselves being created and sustained by him. (*Word Into Silence*, p. 76)

Meditate for thirty minutes.

The way of meditation

Taking the following injunction of St Paul's to heart, I want to explore a few more things about our way of meditating with a mantra.

> And now, my friends, we have one thing to beg and to pray
> of you, by our fellowship with the Lord Jesus. We passed
> on to you the tradition of the way we must live to please
> God; you are indeed already following it, but we beg you to
> do so yet more thoroughly. (1 Thess. 4:1)

Some time ago I heard a programme on the radio about a woman who had been born blind. She was about thirty-five, married and the mother of several young children. She went to see a doctor who thought that some special operation he had developed could give her back some of her sight. She had the operation and to her and the doctor's and everyone's amazement she got perfect sight. She had never seen in her life before, and she was a guest on the radio programme because of the problems that this created for her. For example, a favourite game that her family used to like to play with her and roar with laughter was that they would hold up something like a teacup and they would say 'What is this?' And the mother would say, 'A book.' She would have no idea just from the look of it what it was at all. Then she would say, 'Give it to me.' Once she felt it she realized it was a teacup, obviously. This was a completely new experience for her. Going to the supermarket almost gave her a nervous breakdown when she saw the array of choice on all the shelves. When she wanted to buy something she would still close her eyes and feel it to see if it was the thing she really wanted. She would often come home with packets of soap powder when she had been sent to buy sugar. The most terrifying of her experiences was walking along the street. She would stop at the kerb and look down the street and see a bus coming along. But she would not know what to make of it at all. She was not certain, for example, how quickly it was approaching. She did not know what would happen. So in the end she decided that she would need to take her white stick with her again and stand at the kerbside. Then she would get to know things as they were.

It was a most interesting story and you could vividly imagine that it would be like that for you if you had never had sight. Well now, it is a bit like that when you start to meditate. You come to completely unfamiliar terrain and you have to face all kinds of problems, such as, 'What do I have to do about praying for Aunt Jemima's bunions?' or whatever you have done all your life. And you feel you have to solve all those problems. As they say in America, it is a completely new ball game. And so I want now to try to clarify the practice of meditation for you.

The writers of the Eastern church and the Orthodox tradition – particularly in the Russian tradition – speak of our hearts being asleep. They say that the task of prayer is to awaken the heart; to awaken it above all to the reality of the presence of God's indwelling Spirit. I think there is a real sense in which learning to meditate is learning to become fully awake, fully alive in the Spirit. And we learn that we are, of course, only fully alive when we are fully awake. Consider this in relation to the Buddha. When the Buddha's disciples went to him and asked him, 'Who are you? Are you the all-wise? Are you the almighty? Are you the all-powerful?' The Buddha simply replied, 'I am the one who is awake.' That wakefulness is of the essence of meditation.

Consider the words that Jesus spoke to the disciples in Gethsemane. You remember, he had gone off to pray by himself. As Matthew describes it he went to 'stay awake and pray'. When he came back to the disciples, who had fallen asleep, he said, 'Could you not stay awake and pray with me?' Mark puts a slightly

[47]

different emphasis when he says, 'Could you not be alert and be wakeful?' Meditation, therefore, in the Christian tradition as well, is the process that helps us to move towards a totally wakeful state, by becoming deeply sensitive to the living Spirit of God dwelling within us. Now to achieve this we need to develop a certain skill that is not at all common among our contemporaries: being totally relaxed and totally awake *at the same time*. Most people, I think, find that falling asleep at meditation can be a big problem because once we start to relax we immediately become drowsy.

Saying the mantra is a way staying awake in an alert stillness. And it can be quite a problem even for people in religious communities because our religious response often just parallels our secular experience. Most of us are used to becoming very busy in all our rites and rituals and the saying of prayers. I don't know if any of you have had the same experience in your own homes, but I used to be absolutely terrified when I went to stay in my grandfather's home because everybody would be gathered for the family rosary. Then after the rosary there were interminable prayers added to it. One of my sisters who was deputed to say the rosary one night just stopped at the end and refused to go on to all these prayers and my aunt urged her, 'The prayers! Go on. The prayers!' So – to the horror of all the Kerry people present – my sister added, 'From creepies and crawlies and things that go bump in the night, O Lord, deliver us!' We can be so used to being compulsively busy in our prayers, and multiplying our prayers, that just becoming silent is quite a problem for us. And so we have always got to be *aware* so that we do not just float off into that 'holy-dozy' sort of state of pious dozing, which John Cassian calls the 'pernicious peace' or the 'lethal sleep'.

I want to elaborate a bit on this because I want you to have a clear understanding of it when it happens. There is a real danger here because the religious person likes this pious religiosity, a feeling of being, as I say, slightly stoned in a religious way; but this can become a half-living, limbo state. Do not underestimate the danger: in my experience, certainly among the religious I have met over the years, people can get stranded in this limbo where they just float and do not make any further progress at all in prayer. They never become fully alive. They do not become fully awake to the presence within, which is a waking experience of the living God.

At the root of this unreality is what one could call 'unspiritual religiosity'. It boils down to an evasion of our responsibility to enter fully into the present moment. I am sure you know the great phrase of St Irenaeus that the 'glory of God is Man fully alive'. To be fully alive means we have to respond totally to the reality of the here and now. This is a bigger problem than you might imagine because it is apparently so much easier for Christians to opt for the past. So many Christians seem to prefer a backward projection into the historical life of Christ and to be constantly locked in to it. They lose contact with the living Christ, the Risen Lord, who lives now in our hearts. That seems to me to be one of the great Christian dangers: reducing your prayer to thinking about the historical life of Jesus. What we must do instead is to encounter the living Lord in our own hearts and then find him elsewhere: in our lives and relationships in the living word of Scripture. There is a serious danger to face here just as it can be one of the dangers, for example, about the Stations of the Cross. It is one of the dangers of the sort of piety that gets locked in to 'meditation' upon the historical events of the life of Jesus. That Jesus lived historically is, of course, of supreme importance. I do not deny that for a moment! But the essence of the New Testament is that the Lord Jesus *lives*. The Risen Christ lives in my heart and in your heart. It is with this dimension of his vital and vitalizing presence within me and within you that we must come to read the account of his historical life.

One danger for us as Christians is to be constantly projecting ourselves back into the past. On the other hand we also face another danger. We cultivate a kind of anticipation of the future. We think, 'Well now, I have my daily work to do. I also have all my

[49]

professional responsibility. I have work to keep up with, and I have to keep abreast of what is going on in the world. But one day I will set out to achieve holiness. One day I will have time to live my life in the presence of God. But now I am in this particular group and I must get on with the actual business of living.' This is a kind of spiritual escapism, pure fantasy.

The task of meditation is to concentrate our attention wholly in and on the reality of the present moment. St Paul tells us that this 'now' holds within it Christ's whole design and purpose which is everywhere at work. If you look at the tenses of Paul's verbs – in the letter to the Ephesians, for example – you find this vital sense of the living Christ now at work in the world. As Christians, our task is to be at work with him, in him, and through him. St Gregory wrote of St Benedict, 'He dwelt within himself, always remaining in the presence of his creator, and not allowing his eyes to gaze on distractions.' This is a clear description of our aim in meditation, which is to enter wholly into the actuality of our being. Our task is to be alive and to be alert to the presence of God within our being and to concentrate our whole attention on that presence; and to find in that presence inspiration for everything we are and everything we do.

An essential idea in St Paul is that *now* is the acceptable time. Now is the day of salvation. We cannot be healthily religious if we want to live on past religious capital or future religious development. The significant moment is the present moment. In meditation we seek to enter fully into the *now*, and there to live our lives to the utmost.

We have to be generous and ambitious about the way we live our lives. We must live to the utmost with the risen, ever-living and ever-loving Lord Jesus. One of the principal hazards of our religion today is that we have underestimated the magnificence of our call. To be committed, in the Pauline vision of faith, is to be committed in the present moment and to find ourselves. In order to do so we must take the deep self and the superficial self and get them together in a real state of dynamic equilibrium. This we do by moving away from every image of ourselves, our complex ego, which usually lives anywhere except in the present. By making that decided act of faith in the presence of the living Lord, to put depth and surface identities in harmony, we find within ourselves the present actuality of his risen life; and we find it with all the power to know and love him that that faith creates.

I will sum this up, for now, by saying that *to be* is to be here and now. Our prayer is above all the ratification of our own being. Our prayer has as its primary aim the healing of the open wound of unreality that lies between what we believe and what we know, so that the two become one.

Here is a story that illustrates this point. I heard recently of a Jesuit academic who had been teaching in a university for some years and was due to take a sabbatical year. He thought that he would ask for a year to experience solitude and prayer. And where better than in one of Charles de Foucauld's hermitages in North Africa? All his colleagues were shaking their heads: 'The poor guy has gone a bit cracked.' He set off anyway to North Africa leaving his books, his theses, his seminars, lectures, and journals all behind him. But when he got to the hermitage he was surprised to find only utter desolation of spirit, utter desolation of mind. Every natural and rational voice inside him urged him to return to civilization without delay, that this was a total waste of time; he must get back to his real world. But fortunately he stuck it out.

If you have ever been in the desert you know its wonderful power to bring you to sanity – eventually. He went out from his hermitage on those vast starlit nights of the desert and he was gradually filled with a sense of the absolute immensity of reality. As he looked at the sky into its endless distance, he saw the grandeur of it all, and the infinite generosity of the scale on which the whole creation is planned. As he did so, his own spirit was flooded with a sense of the real and immediate presence of God. When he stood outside his hermitage and looked at the marvel of that sky, it was a moment of conversion for him. This sense of God's creative power and the infinite scale of God's presence brought with it an experience of immense peace, a peace that comes from finding the essence of things. He had found by his experience that God was *all in all*. He said that this brought with it a sense of perspective which he described as a sense of Godliness. He had been converted by finding God in silence, in stillness, in a place beyond all distraction. And from this experience he returned to his university convinced in knowledge, rather than theory, of the great liberating power that is released when we know and experience the primacy of the fact of God: that God IS.

I think every Christian is called to an experience of this kind – a dying to self in the desert, a dying that is painful, a dying that requires nerve, perseverance, and persistence, a dying that is the only possible way to resurrection, to a new life in the Spirit. For most of us what corresponds to the Charles de Foucauld hermitage is what the Russian Orthodox Church calls the 'Pilgrimage to the Heart'. That phrase well describes our own meditation pilgrimage which is the way of the mantra. Just as the Jesuit was tempted to return to his books, his work, his reputation, his career, and so forth, we, when we are on our pilgrimage, are often lured back to our thoughts, our cleverness, our minds, our daydreams. The one quality that we require to arrive at the goal is simply perseverance.

I want to emphasize for you that the perseverance required is a perseverance in being open to the prayer of Jesus. Our theology of prayer offers us a whole literature to show that God is the prime mover. The ultimate prayer is the prayer of Jesus. It is not *our* prayer at all. 'We do not even know how we ought to pray' (Rom. 8:26). God is the giver of all gifts in prayer. That is what we must always remember. We cannot twist his arm or force him to do anything by resorting to techniques of breathing or sitting or saying mantras or anything else. God is the prime mover. But what we can do is to dispose ourselves to receive his gift which is always the gift of Himself.

The essential disposition for prayer is to be alive, to be awake, to be alert, to be ready. This is where our meditation has its place. Meditation teaches us to be ready, to deepen our wakefulness, and to sharpen our alertness. The Jesuit knew *about* God before he set out to his desert and persevered there. And before he went to the desert his 'notional experience' of God was impressive. It was impressive enough to make him a career and a reputation as a theologian of some emminence. But in the desert, as we in our pilgrimage, he came to realize what he had always half-suspected as he wrote his learned articles, that it is one thing to know *about* God but it is quite another thing to know and love him directly, and to experience ourselves as directly known and loved. It is this increasing awareness of the inadequacy of our ordinary knowledge of God and of our experience of him that leads us to meditate and to persevere.

I would like to end this session with a stanza from a poem by the Sufi poet Atta. It is from his book *The Parliament of Birds*.

> Come, you lost atoms to your centre draw,
> and be the eternal mirror that you saw.
> Rays that have wandered into darkness wide,
> return and back into your sun subside.

Questions for Reflection:
1. 'Meditation is a completely new ballgame.'
How does the practice of meditation differ from other prayer practices I learned in the past?

2. 'The ultimate prayer is the prayer of Jesus.'
How does meditation challenge my vision of prayer?

3. How does the practice of meditation integrate my awareness of the historical Jesus with my experience of the present Christ?

4. What is the challenge to persevere, in my experience of meditation?

Application:
The grandeur of nature shows the infinite generosity of our Creator. Let me better appreciate my natural surroundings every day.

> The experience of transcendence ... occurs within the nature of things – our nature – the parables of the kingdom show that the essence of experience is natural growth. A small mustard seed grows into a tree big enough for the birds to come and roost in its branches. To try to make it grow faster or slower would be absurd and counterproductive. It is the same when we experience the growth of the Kingdom in our hearts as we follow the journey of meditation. Day by day we let the husk of the ego drop away and like a seed we die to self that we may fulfill the destiny that is our true meaning, that the potential of life within us may come to full fruition. (*Letters from the Heart*, pp. 70, 71)

Meditate for thirty minutes.

Jesus the teacher

Let us examine the teachings of Jesus as presented in the Gospel of Matthew. They present us with a clear vision of the absoluteness of the Kingdom of God.

If people are often hindered from entering the Kingdom it is in no small part due to the Pharisaical teachers, the false prophets preventing them or misleading them. But Jesus also says that every one of us must accept the personal responsbility to understand the absoluteness of the demand that this entry into the Kingdom involves for all. No one can read the Gospel of Matthew without seeing how frank and uncompromising Jesus is. It is not as though we have to pay an entrance fee at the gate in order to get into the Kingdom. We have to pay, instead, with our very selves. That is the payment: the fullness of everything that we are.

And in spite of the fact that Jesus tells us that we will be rewarded a hundredfold even in this life, still we hang back. 'No servant can be the slave of two masters,' he says. 'You cannot serve God and Mammon. Therefore, I tell you put away anxious thought about food and drink to keep you alive' (Matthew 6:24-5, author's translation).

And so Jesus tells us not only to abandon attachment and anxiety regarding material things and not place our hope and confidence in them, but also not even to think about them. The same holds true for interior possessions. This is the 'narrow gate' that is so central to his teaching.

> Enter by the narrow gate. The gate is wide that leads to perdition, there is plenty of room on the road, and many go

that way; but the gate that leads to life is small and the road
is narrow, and those who find it are few. (Matthew 7:13–14)

That is why in our meditation we concentrate the whole of our
attention on the Lord Jesus. Attention is as narrow as a laser beam,
but it leads to life. If we can only concentrate our whole attention
on the Lord, then the whole of creation opens up already enlightened by this light – enlightened by the Lord who *is* light and life.

The main point that we are concentrating on during this retreat
is that we have got to leave self behind – and that we *can*. You
know, perhaps, from your studies of Scripture, that this image of
the narrow gate is taken from the narrow entrance in the city wall
of a Middle Eastern town. The camel loaded with the goods of the
rich man just cannot get through it. The camel has to be unloaded
before it can get through into the market. Jesus used this metaphor
because people saw the reality of it every day on their daily rounds.
We cannot get through into this central place where all the goods
are laid out, where the riches of the kingdom of God are to be
found, unless we first unload our *self* of all our baggage. And that
is the power of Jesus to teach us and to show us how to do it. 'If
anyone wishes to be a follower of mine, he must leave self behind'
(Matthew 16:24).

It is important to understand that although Jesus preaches perfection he is not fanatical. He accepts that there are stages of perfection through which we must all pass on our way to this absolute
surrender of self. In the story of the rich young man who asked
what else he should do to inherit eternal life apart from keeping the
commandments, Jesus showed him that the renunciation of wealth
was only the beginning of perfection. It was a point of departure
for this absolute surrender. And so he said, 'If you wish to go the
whole way, go, sell your possessions, and give to the poor, and then
you will have riches in heaven; and come follow me' (Matthew
19:21). Now we all look at this in our very materialistic way: that
perfection was to sell your possessions. And Jesus is saying this is

[56]

only the first step. If you want to follow me, fine. But first get rid of all the extraneous baggage in your life and *then* come follow me. That poverty of spirit which we experience within ourselves while saying the mantra will prepare us to read Scripture with a much more alert and more sensitive perception. That poverty is also our way of dispossession.

The keynote of Jesus' preaching about perfection is this surrender of self in letting go. He does not ask us to do it in any solemn or complex way. The essence is simplicity itself. 'I tell you this: unless you turn round and become like children, you will never enter the kingdom of heaven' (Matt. 18:3).

I met an old friend of mine yesterday. He soldiered with me in Malaya and is a doctor in Belfast now, and he was asking me what I was doing – was I on holiday? And I said, 'Oh no, I'm giving a thirty-day retreat.'

And he said, 'My gosh! How could you possibly give a retreat for thirty days?' He said, 'Douglas (my name before I became a monk was Douglas), what are you telling those good people?'

I thought about that and said, 'Well, the main thing I can tell them is that there is nothing to tell them!' And that is the keynote again of Jesus' preaching. It is about this childlike simplicity that allows us to open our hearts to Jesus in a completely childlike and trusting way. And so Jesus links perfection with poverty. All of us today seem to find great difficulty in understanding this idea of poverty and simplicity. I think anyone can understand it if they can learn to root the mantra in their heart. The poverty of practising meditation is the poverty of renouncing all concern for your self at the innermost centre of your being. Secondly, there is the the utter simplicity of the practice. It is a childlike, complete trust in the Lord. Those are the two points that I would like you to get absolutely clear in your mind and heart: simplicity and poverty. Maybe that was what I should have told my old friend I was telling you!

When we consider the life of Jesus, we are taught to be very honest about what all this involves. He says in his proclamation of the gospel that the attainment of these qualities will involve suffering and we have to be prepared for that. He warns that once these qualities have been gained to any real degree, they will bring his followers persecution because his followers then will be like him, telling the truth to those who do not want to hear it. 'My brothers,' St John wrote to the early Christians, 'do not be surprised if the world hates you' (1 John 2:13). In fact, we ought to be pleased. What Jesus tells us, however, is that the suffering that is involved in the following of his gospel is not negative. In fact it is nothing compared to the joy of being with him and going with him to the Father.

We must be very clear about the absoluteness of what Jesus is inviting us to. This is at the heart of the man and his message: Jesus as a teacher of prayer.

There is no doubt, as you look at the New Testament and the understanding of the new gospel in the early church, that Jesus was in his own day everything that we would today understand and describe in popular language as a *guru*, a teacher. He lived a hidden life for thirty years before his active ministry. The Gospel account of his life suggests that he had deep rabbinical learning, after a long period of preparation. And there was then the preparatory purifying trial in the desert for forty days. And during his ministry, there were regular periods of solitude when he withdrew from the crowds to be alone with his heavenly Father.

Jesus was everywhere addressed as 'Rabbi', which is the Hebrew word for teacher. Perhaps the most revealing line in the whole of the Scripture identifying Jesus as the teacher is in the Gospel of Luke when the disciples turn to him and say, 'Lord, teach us to pray, as John taught his disciples' (Luke 11:2). It is important to understand that Jesus did not teach new, esoteric techniques of prayer. He did not suggest any magic formula. The Lord's prayer itself is not some sort of magic spell. But because he was not only a teacher but a prophet, he came to recall people to prayer in the ground of their being not just to restore ancient rites or customs from which people had fallen away. Jesus' point about external prayer is that people fall into these rites far more than they fall away from them. He was recalling people to the basic, necessary attitude concerning God as the most significant and important relationship in our life – in all human life. For Jesus this attitude was not a matter of words or formulas, but of the experience of our complete and utter dependence upon God. The attitudes that he denounced with the strongest passion were wordiness, formalism, and pedantry, which alienate us from the basic experience of our dependence upon God.

Jesus taught that prayer is an interior dimension of our relationship with the Father. We are told that we must not make a show of our religion, so in the Gospel of Matthew he says:

> When you pray, do not be like the hypocrites; they love to say their prayers standing up in the synagogue and at the street-corners, for everyone to see them. I tell you this: they have their reward already. But when you pray, go into a room by yourself, shut the door, and pray to your Father who is there in the secret place; and your Father who sees what is secret will reward you. (Matt. 6:5–6)

In telling us to pray by ourselves, Jesus is using the Jewish hyperbolic style of contrast, warning against the dangers of ceremonial prayer, or liturgy, which can so easily become mere formalism, or religious vanity. But we should not ignore the literal truth at the heart of the hyperbole. What he is saying, if I understand it correctly, is that prayer is the personal responsibility of each individual. We have to take the responsibility of going to our own private room, to the innermost chamber of our heart. Only in accepting that responsbility in the direct encounter with one's own self will we meet the Father in the secret place. Jesus is saying that it is this meeting of the Father in the innermost chamber of our heart that gives us something that we can share with others in the liturgical prayer, in a group of realized spiritual people who come together to share their joy in their holding the Lord in their hearts. So we must understand the dynamic balance in the teaching of Jesus. In establishing the Eucharist, and in saying that he would be present where two or three were gathered in his name, he certainly did not forget or forbid sacramental prayer or community worship but, as in every other aspect of his message, Jesus gives primary and permanent importance to direct, personal experience and to the integrity of responsible persons.

After establishing this priority, Jesus is shown warning his followers against seeing prayer as a self-centred experience. It becomes self-centred rather than God-centred whenever we think of ourselves at the time of our prayer – like those too sure of their own goodness and who look down on everybody else; or like the Pharisee praying in the temple thanking God that he was not like others; or like those who are wholly taken up with their emotional needs or their anxiety about food and drink and clothes. Jesus is saying that there is always this tendency to self-centred prayer and we must all recognize it. There is also the danger that if people go off to their room to pray in the secret chamber of their heart, they could look as if they are being self-centred. But Jesus tells us that we *must* be with our heavenly Father in our personal solitude. During our prayer that is where our attention must be, not on how we seem to others.

It seems to me, from reading the Gospels, that the solution of Jesus to avoid the universal tendency to self-centred prayer is a very simple one: to restrict our use of words, because it is in language, above all, that we express and enshrine our self-fascination. When we do this in prayer we inevitably increase our self-fascination by the spectacle of ourselves addressing the Almighty God and, as it were, holding God entranced in our own personality; holding God's special attention as we discuss with him our personal problems or our virtues. So what has Jesus said?

> In your prayers do not go babbling on like the heathen,
> who imagine that the more they say the more likely they are
> to be heard. Do not imitate them. Your Father knows what
> your needs are before you ask him. (Matt. 6:7–8)

Jesus is quite clearly discouraging us from multiplying words in our prayer. He is encouraging us instead to use a form of prayer that is consistent with his general warning that 'unless you turn around and become like children, you will never enter the kingdom of heaven' (Matt. 18:3). The supreme example Jesus puts before us of simplicity in prayer is the tax collector who is contrasted with the self-satisfied Pharisee. The publican or tax collector 'kept his distance and would not even raise his eyes to heaven, but beat upon his breast, saying, "O God, have mercy on me, sinner that I am"' It was this man, I tell you, and not the other, who went home acquitted of his sins' (Luke 18:13). As you know, the Russian Orthodox church takes its mantra, the Jesus Prayer, from this chapter. The point of the story is that simple repetitive prayer is born of humility and of a recognition of the power of God to forgive sin. This is what the Lord Jesus puts before us as the ideal. Jesus constantly stresses that we must pray to the Father, and praying *with him* as he prays to the Father – going to the Father *with* him, *in* him, *through* him – is the heart of Christian prayer and its meaning.

The teaching of Jesus on prayer is that it is a personal responsibility. Each of us must accept the challenge of being and of discovering unity within ourselves, union with the creator of the universe. Prayer demands our complete trust and simplicity. It requires us to be receptive to the presence of the divine life within us. It is essentially a natural process of growth and development, requiring on our part sensitivity, openness, and perseverance.

If we are invited to renounce ourselves completely in order to find our real selves, then we have to understand that Jesus is calling us, above all, to be open to the reality of our creation. This call

[61]

is a call to an increasingly acute attentiveness and wonder at the reality of our being. Jesus spoke often of the need to sustain this attentiveness, this wakefulness, and all the more as his own personal crisis drew near. The final words of his ministry before his passion were, 'Keep awake then; for you do not know on what day your Lord is to come ... Hold yourselves ready, therefore, because the Son of Man will come at the time you least expect him' (Matt. 24:42, 44). This message is repeated again in the parable of the foolish and wise virgins: 'Keep awake then; for you never know the day or the hour' (Matt. 25:13). The parable of the talents holds the same message. Now all these teachings on waiting and being awake have an eschatological dimension: when the Son of man comes in all his glory he must find us up and awake. And yet they are also a present experience, an experience that is part of our patient attentiveness in meditation day by day.

I want to stress again a word about the 'pernicious peace' of John Cassian. When we hear the words of Jesus about the absolute demand of the Kingdom, when we look at our own personal responsibility for making this pilgrimage ourselves, and when we look at his constant call to wakefulness, it appears clear that Jesus is the guru in the full tradition of the Eastern masters. He constantly speaks about the basic religious experience as an awakening, an enlightenment, a self-realization. Now this is what we have to say to the world: that within the mystery of the most Holy Trinity we awaken to the fact that the Lord Jesus prays within us; his spirit is within us, and he takes us to the Father. Awakening to this reality is our enlightenment. And this experience of awakening and enlightenment is the basic experience of vitalization that Jesus came to communicate to us: 'I have come that men may have life, and may have it in all its fullness' (John 10:10).

Questions for Reflection:
1. 'Put away anxious thought about food and drink to keep you alive.'
Not only food and drink cause me anxiety. What aspects of my life
bring fear, distraction or possessiveness?

2. 'Enter by the narrow gate.'
What 'baggage' causes me to travel with unnecessary burdens?
How can I simplify my life and make my travel lighter?

3. How does meditation help me to 'leave self behind'?

4. How does the solitary aspect of meditation complement the
communal aspect of liturgy? What is unique about both acts of
prayer? What do they share in common?

Application:
I will simplify those areas in my life that are cluttered with distractions. I will practise gratitude for the gifts God has given me, both
material and spiritual. I will meditate each morning and evening as
a way to help to come to simple wonder.

> The faithful saying of our mantra is our response to this call
> of Jesus. It is work – the work of God. Above all, meditation
> is an all-out onslaught on egoism, on isolation and on sad-
> ness. It is an affirmation of consciousness and life through
> the experience of love. The Christian vision demands a
> community that is created and vitalized in the mind of
> Christ. The message this community must communicate is
> that it is possible for all of us to become alive with the life of
> Christ. It is not only possible, it is the destiny of each one
> of us. (*The Present Christ*, p. 88)

Meditate for thirty minutes.

Encounter with Jesus

This is a remarkable statement about reality from the letter to the Galatians:

> To prove that you are sons, God has sent into our hearts the Spirit of his Son, crying 'Abba! Father!' You are therefore no longer a slave but a son, and if a son, then also by God's own act an heir.
>
> For through faith you are all sons of God in union with Christ Jesus. Baptized into union with him, you have all put on Christ as a garment. (Gal. 4:6–7; 3:26–7)

How can we come to understand that reality more clearly? What we gradually find is that our daily practice of meditation leads to the fullness of the life of Christ within us. In saying our mantra we just allow ourselves to mature, to become fully ourselves, so that our encounter with the Lord Jesus may itself be a fully personal and fully mature encounter. What we have to do – in the language of the East – is to realize ourselves, to become fully ourselves. I think it is true to say that in the modern world fewer and fewer people do really know themselves or feel in touch with themselves. If you multiply enough distractions in your life you need never even address that question of who you really and truly are. Not to know yourself is one of the tragic inadequacies of much Christian living. In every loving relationship there are at least two persons involved and so there is always this dynamic movement from the lover to the beloved. The consummation of this loving exchange of self is the holy, simple communion where each loses himself in the other. The extraordinary thing about our call to holiness is that

Jesus loses himself in us. The loving relationship is fully loving on his side too.

We have to be very clear that in the Christian life, the response is always *from* us as a result of the initiative taken by God. That is a very important order to bear in mind. 'The love I speak of is not our love for God but the love he showed us in sending us his Son' (1 John 4:10). In many religions the essential religious act involves humanity moving to God. In the Christian religion the deepest religious actions are always those of God stooping down moving into humanity. As long as our faith is seen as comprising only the movement from human beings to God, we remain self-centred and earthbound. The gift of meditation is that what we are learning to be still, to be silent, to be aware, so that the Lord Jesus may manifest himself to us and within us and so that his love may become self-realized in us. What we discover in deep prayer is that we ourselves are caught up in the movement of the love of the Lord Jesus returning to his Father. That is how we achieve our own self-transcendence. We are quite literally taken out of ourselves in a movement of ecstasy. Another name for this movement is love.

Something I have often tried to stress is that we must understand our own loveableness. The first step to full personhood and to full maturity is that we allow ourselves to be loved. So often, we keep others at a distance. This is precisely why the Lord Jesus has sent us his Holy Spirit into our hearts: to touch us, to awaken us, and to draw us into the redemptive light of that love of Jesus. Remember the words of Richard of St Victor that as we meditate we become increasingly aware of the love of the Lord Jesus. We *feel* the love of the Lord Jesus. And then we see a great light enlightening the whole of our being and we know it to be the divine light.

It is extraordinary, but I am sure you have come across it in your own lives, that so many people are reluctant to allow themselves to be loved, because the level of fearfulness is so deeply implanted in their hearts. This is why I stress that our experience

[65]

in prayer is of the Risen Jesus and this experience opens us to his fullness of life and freedom. It is the Lord we meet in our prayer. Jesus – who has transcended every limitation of the human condition – including all the limitations of fear, ignorance, loneliness, guilt, and rejection. The totally free and human, totally loving person Jesus lives in our hearts. He lives in an entirely personal, loving relationship with us. What he calls us to is full consciousness of his presence. That is what it means to be a Christian: to be converted to his presence, to be fully conscious of the life of the loving Lord Jesus within our heart.

We need always to remember that Jesus *has* become become fully awake, fully conscious of the love of his Father, and we are called to the same consciousness, to exactly the same love. The tragedy of so much Christianity over the centuries has been that we have terribly underestimated our calling. In awakening to the love of the Lord Jesus we awaken to complete communion with all creation in the life of Jesus in the Father. Some meditators believe that if we could get one per cent of the people of the world to meditate we would solve the problems that confront humanity. I think there is a lot of truth in that. One example is the environmental problem. If we understood our communion with the forests and the rivers and the mountains and the plains we could not treat them in the shameful and barbarous way that we do. We must enter into a loving relationship with our environment; and if we do not, we are doomed: that love is itself part of the love which Jesus has awakened to and shares with us

I want to stress the magnitude of what we are about. We are not just talking about something that will bring us a little peace of mind or make us a little bit more efficient in doing our job. We are talking about coming to a full awareness of our own place in creation: about our personal relationship with the Creator, with all creation and all created beings. That is why we can say that meditation is the principal road to humility: because, through meditation, we understand our own place in creation and our relationships within the cosmos. And we understand that a loving Trinity is at the centre of all creation.

We begin awakening to all this with a very dim awareness of the stirring of the Spirit in our heart. All we have to do is to be simple and faithful and say our mantra. As we look back on our journey of meditation, that we could never say at what moment this awareness became clear in our minds and hearts. But what we are increasingly aware of is that as we continue to say our mantra, humbly and faithfully, the world around us is gradually transformed because the heart within us is totally transformed, transfigured by the love of the Lord.

We must understand that every one of us is called to a spriitual maturity in which we become 'alive with the life of God' (1 Peter 4:6). We do this not by thinking about God, not by imagining God, not by inventing imaginary conversations with him. We do it by allowing his presence to become the sole reality in our consciousness. Prayer is the life of the Spirit of Jesus within the human heart, the Spirit in whom we are incorporated in the Body of Christ, the Spirit which takes each one of us fully awakened to the Father. Prayer is awakening to this Spirit in all its fullness in our heart.

I do not think there are forms or methods of prayer; there is only *prayer*. I like to think of that prayer as the stream of love between the Spirit of the Risen Jesus and his Father, the stream of love in which we are incorporate. Similarly, once you begin to pray you pray always. There is no part-time prayer or partial prayer. The Spirit is always alive in our heart, and that stream of love is always a reality in our heart. Then our times of meditation, our times of prayer, are simply times when we make this complete turn of consciousness to the ever-present Reality. The more you give yourself to this, plunging deeply into this stream of love, the more you become aware of what St Paul meant when he called us to pray without ceasing. This is the state that is also called enlightenment, when the awareness of the reality of the love of Jesus for his Father is constant in our hearts. Insofar as we can be analytical about this, what we are aware of is our total poverty, our total dependence upon the sustaining love of God and our infinite enrichment in that love.

I have been talking to you about a journey – about a pilgrimage. The pilgrimage is to the source level of our own being. We are on that pilgrimage as long as we say our mantra with simplicity and persevere in our poverty – renouncing thought, imagination and, ultimately, our own self-consciousness. As the mantra becomes rooted more and more deeply in us, and more thoroughly integrated in our consciousness, so our whole being participates in a single, unified response to the Spirit. The journey leads us to an integration of our selfhood where every part of our being is activated and involved in the same loving, harmonious response to the Father. Our aim is to accept fully the salvation that Jesus has achieved for us: the total deliverance from everything that is isolating: total union with the whole of creation. What we discover is our own essential unity. And we discover, too, our absolute freedom to soar to the Father.

Do not let me mislead you with rhetoric. There is no doubt about the absolute demand of the mantra. There is a real sense in which saying the mantra is such an act of pure faith that it amounts to religious recklessness because it is, in essence, our total acceptance of the reality of God's love flooding our inmost heart through the Spirit of the Risen Jesus. It calls us to die to self. It takes an act of absolute renunciation to throw ourselves completely upon the love of Jesus. It is only that absolute renunciation and faith, however, that allows us to rise in his power, to share his authority, and above all to communicate his love.

We cannot manufacture or anticipate this experience; it is a gift of God. All we can do is learn to be still, to be silent and to wait. As we learn that stillness and silence, as we learn to wait, we do so with an ever-growing sense of our own potential and of our own harmony. But we must be patient. In God's time we will experience the flooding of our heart with the love of Jesus and we will be ready to respond to his summons when it comes. It is a summons that asks us to respond to the fullness of our own personhood in our encounter with Jesus. Every member in the church, as I understand it, is called to this. Every member of the human race is called to this awakening. Our great responsibility is to wake up, to be ready, to be at the disposition of the Father, and then in humility and love to bring the glory of that wakefulness, the enlightenment of that wakefulness to all humankind.

I would like to reflect for a bit on the role of the teacher in meditation. The teacher's main aim and objective is to phase himself or herself out as soon as possible. The only teacher is the Lord Jesus. The teacher is simply there to point the way, not to make people dependent upon him- or herself. The whole purpose of meditation is to make us entirely free to soar to our heavenly Father. The teacher has the basic rôle of telling you in five minutes what has to be done, and encouraging you thereafter to continue. If you want to teach someone to meditate at some time in the future, the only way is to meditate with them. That is where the teacher is at his or her best: in absolute silence with his or her disciple. It is important to understand that. On the question of what the teacher can do, the best chance that you have, as far as I know, is to find a master and to meditate with him for whatever time is available to you, whether it it is six months or a year or two years.

One of the great contemporary masters in the East was Sri Ramana Maharshi, who died in 1955. If anyone came to him he always said that he had nothing to say; he would love to be silent with whoever came. As far as I know, Sri Ramana never wrote a book, never wrote anything except a few hymns, and yet he was probably one of the greatest of modern teachers. He was the silent teacher of the French Catholic monk, Swami Abhishiktananda, himself a great teacher.

I think in general, the less you say about what happens during meditation, the better. Discussions about what happens when

[69]

someone meditates are entirely counter-productive. There are times when it might be appropriate for you to approach your teacher and say you are having this or that particular experience or difficulty. It might well be that he would tell you to ignore it, or say your mantra, or whatever. That would probably be what he would say in ninety per cent of the cases. I could see occasions where some deeper analysis of the precise problem could be appropriate. But that would be for the judgement of the teacher. The general principle is: the less analysis, the less talking about it, the better.

People have a wonderful capacity to get hold of the wrong end of the stick and so they can get into difficulties which are totally unnecessary. Perhaps sometimes, in helping others who are learning to meditate, you need to find out what they have been doing, and to do that you may – in certain circumstances – have to do a certain amount of analysis to see what exactly has happened. But that would be minimal, and the less analysis the better. That is where the art of the teacher comes in: to synthesize, not analyse.

Questions for Reflection:
1. Are my relationships marked by love or by possessiveness? How can I be more loving?

2. Is my relationship with nature loving or exploitative?

3. The teacher's main aim and objective is to phase himself or herself out of the picture. What teachers have I known in my life? What characteristics attracted me to them?

Application:
I will strive to make my relationships with others and with nature less selfish and more selfless.

In meditation we develop our capacity to turn our whole being towards the Other. We learn to let our neighbour be just as we learn to let God be. We learn not to manipulate our neighbour but rather to reverence him, to reverence his importance, the wonder of his being; in other words, we learn to love him. Because of this, prayer is the great school of community. In and through a common seriousness and perseverance in prayer we realize the true glory of Christian community as a fraternity of the anointed, living together in profound and loving mutual respect. (*Word Into Silence*, p. 78)

Meditate for thirty minutes.

Climate of prayer

Let us take this reading from the Gospel of St Mark as our guide
for this session:

> Then he called the people to him, as well as his disciples,
> and said to them, 'Anyone who wishes to be a follower of
> mine must leave self behind; he must take up his cross, and
> come with me. Whoever cares for his own safety is lost; but
> if a man will let himself be lost for my sake and for the
> Gospel, that man is safe. What does a man gain by winning
> the whole world at the cost of his true self?' (Mark 8:34–6)

The most important thing for all of us is that we really do learn
to be with Jesus; that we really do learn that Jesus is with us and
everything else in our life must take second place to this primary
relationship. The key to the whole realization of our potentiality is
leaving self behind in relationship.

I want to explore the contemporary climate that contributes to
the making of each one of us. I want to start with this statement for
us to consider: The church, like Jesus, exists for others, and its
power and effectiveness is in direct proportion to its selflessness,
its self-transcendence. Since *we are* the church, our power, our
effectiveness in proclaiming the gospel of Jesus and the reality of
the Risen Jesus to the world is in direct proportion to our
selflessness, to our capacity to take the searchlight of consciousness off ourselves and to put it on the Lord Jesus. It is only in this
spiritual state of being other-centred – which to the world is utter
foolishness – the church itself can really believe what it is meant to
proclaim. If we want to speak – and we must – with authoritative

voices about Jesus, and communicate him and his gospel, then we have to be in a way of being which is other-centred, neighbour-centred, Jesus-centred, God-centred. It is only then that we will be genuinely experiencing in the centre of our being the loving dynamic of the Good News. And the Good News is that Jesus has set us free, that we possess the liberty of the children of God, and that we are free to love him with every power of our being. We are free to communicate his love to the whole world.

I think this is so tremendously important because what we have to proclaim to the world is not a past experience – even something so wonderful as the past experience of Jesus himself dying on the cross and redeeming us. But we are not proclaiming a past experience; we are proclaiming a present reality. And that present reality is the reality of the glorified Lord Jesus present in our hearts. That is the Good News. The Lord Jesus lives in our hearts in his resurrected and glorious mode of being.

The church can only proclaim what it is in the state of experiencing. Or to put it differently, the church can only proclaim what it is. We are the church and our responsibility and our opportunity is to proclaim that power of the Lord Jesus as a living reality. But we can only speak of what we know; we can only be what we are. The state of being that we are summoned to by Jesus is the state of being other-centred, which is, of course, being in a state of prayer.

Because of the pluralism of the world we live in, it is difficult to generalize about the church. The church is in all states of being and at all levels of reality. We have got South American guerilla priests. We have got the international charismatic movement. We have got followers of Archbishop Lefebvre. What we have all got to accept is our own level of responsibility. If we are going to be effective proclaimers of the word of God in the world today it will be so only insofar as each one of us puts the Lord Jesus first in our own lives. If we are going to proclaim the gospel, then the gospel must first have called us to an encounter and communion with the reality of God's power at work in creation: a call which is effected by the power of the redeeming, sacrificial love of Jesus. The fundamental reality of all levels of being and of the church is interpenetrated with the love and reality of the Holy Spirit.

The danger for each of us, and for the church, is that instead of being turned outward to the Lord Jesus and to his path, we are constantly considering ourselves or the place of the church in the world today. It is because we are not looking outward, but are fearfully concerned with our own image, our own structures, our own organization, that the church is seen by so many today as irrelevant and ineffective. This is happening at a time when the general consciousness of all societies in the world has never been more keenly attuned to the basic need of the stabilizing power of the enduring spiritual realities.

In my travels around the world it has often struck me that the church today is like a power company trying to light a city with candles while, right in the midst of the city, there is a power source that would enlighten the whole city and the surrounding countryside. That power is the power of the Lord Jesus in our hearts. This is what each of us has to find – how we can be united to this power source so that we can be light and refreshment and joy to our society. Men and women living in the world are coming more and more to realize the importance of recognizing some enduring spiritual reality at the heart of their personal and social lives. Our opportunity as Christians is to show that reality right in our own hearts. What we have got to do is to find the right frequency, as it were, to send out a signal to our lost contemporaries, so as to draw them into the universal family of the Lord Jesus, the family created by love and fed by truth. We must understand with as great a clarity as possible that that frequency is nothing other than the life of the risen Lord vital in the heart of every being. And it joins all of us into the conscious awareness of itself.

We must deepen our understanding of the church because the church is composed of those who know this life at the very centre of their being, which is also the centre of all being. This is to

[74]

understand that the church is the living and glorified Lord Jesus. And we must understand, too, that the world has a right to expect from us confidence and authority as we proclaim this reality out of our own experience. It is just this authentic knowledge that our contemporaries in the world are searching for. This is the personal knowledge and experience that St Paul was constantly exhorting the early church to acquire and to deepen.

Let me develop this idea more fully. St Paul speaks of knowledge. It seems to me that what our contemporaries are seeking for is a knowledge which transcends the transient and immediate; a knowledge that gives meaning to our whole life, to all that we are. St Paul pointed out to the early Christians that this is something we have to be deeply serious about – not solemn, but serious. Seriousness will make each one of us ready for the difficulties involved. We, the church, and the world need discipline and patience, faithfulness to the pilgrimage, if we are going to set out on the path of prayer and persevere on our journey. Prayer – our encounter in the Lord, our discovery of his power and his love at work in our heart – must be the first priority of our life.

I travel around quite a bit talking with laity, priests, and religious. Everywhere I go I find a sincere desire for prayer, a sincere desire to find the way back. But everywhere, too, I find that the discipline required to find our way back brings a kind of sadness: 'I would like to do it, but …'

As we know, the Lord Jesus asks us to follow him freely, with liberty. He asks us to follow him wholly, with our whole heart. 'Anyone who wishes to be a follower of mine must leave self behind.' The knowledge of God that St Paul speaks of cannot be gained in the way we acquire a knowledge of history or economics or thermodynamics. There is no such thing really as a course on prayer or a course on spirituality. In all the courses we take there are just so many facts, ideas, and theories that we add to our memory banks. But these facts and theories are mere possessions that can not fully enter into the mystery of our personhood. The real

[75]

knowledge that St Paul speaks of is of a totally different order because it is the knowledge where the centre of consciousness, the
intelligent agent, is not ourselves acquiring, savouring, experiencing, or observing. The knowledge that St Paul speaks of is not
something we possess but something that possesses us. And here
is the marvel of the Christian mystery with which we are entrust-
ed. We are taken up into the mystery of the Godhead itself. In
terms of Christian theology we know fully only because we have
been fully understood. Here again is the freeing power of the
gospel of Jesus. In his love we are truly known; we are fully taken
into the mystery of the Godhead. We can never be fully free just by
knowing. We can only know fully when we are completely known.

The strange but redeeming feature of our rather mad world
today is that somehow so many of the young people – perhaps the
not-so-young, too – are being led to the threshold of this most sensitive and most beautiful spiritual perception: that we can only
fully know when we are fully known. We can only be fully known
when we leave self behind and so allow the other to know us. The
extraordinary thing that I encounter when talking to college and
university students is that they are living in a culture that has almost lost its literacy and at times almost its potential for intelligent
communication. But the students have somehow or other often
managed to grasp, with a sureness greater than that of many pre-
ceding generations, that it is only in allowing ourselves to be
known that we can fully know. I cannot imagine any other generation, for example, in which Thomas Merton's book *Zen and the
Birds of Appetite* would have become a bestseller among the
young. I do not think that in any other generation, apart perhaps
from the time of St Francis, that so many have focussed so fear-
lessly on those central words of the message of Jesus that the one
who would find his life must lose it.

There are tremendous signs of hope in today's world and in
today's church. The church is oceanic. It rises and swells in places
as it recedes in others. Those who have left self behind to follow

[76]

Christ have left the shore and are carried on the ocean, moved by the tide and the ground swell. The great prayer movement that has arisen in the church in recent years is one of the great signs of hope. The charismatic houses of prayer, and the contemplative groups and centres, all point in different ways to the same phenomenon: an urgent spiritual hunger. It seems to me that today we have a special opportunity and a special responsibility to make our communities into communities of prayer because *we* are men and women of prayer. And because we *are* the atmosphere, the orientation and the priority of our communities are rooted in and founded on the the love and presence of the living Lord Jesus.

One of the things that I find among the young is a veneration for the great religious personalities of our day who express the gospel in their words and deeds and way of being – men and women like Mother Teresa, Cardinal Suenens, Jean Vanier – people with real enthusiasm – *en theos* – with the indwelling God powerfully transforming them at the centre of their being. These great personalities testify to the central power of Christian conviction. The power is this: that once the inner commitment or conversion has taken place, then we are not working for the eradication of our personality but for the fulfilment of our personhood. What we have to show our contemporaries as Christians is that if only we have the courage to lose our life will we indeed joyfully find it. This is the message that we have to proclaim and to communicate to those with whom we live and work. The central message in the preaching of Jesus is that he came to bring us life, life in all its fullness.

I want to close this session by putting one more idea before you. The task for us as simple Christians is for each one of us to see ourselves and to experience ourselves as the church we speak of. We each must come to know ourselves as the presence of the living Christ in our world. This is the consciousness and response of all the great figures of the church. We must understand the situation that we find ourselves in and to respond to it fully,

[77]

courageously, and generously. We have to learn to see the church not as some multinational company or international organization. We have to learn to see it as the living Body of Christ. We can only do it if we continuously re-discover ourselves as personal temples of the Holy Spirit. We have to see ourselves as the redeemed and loved of Jesus. Seeing who we are, we can then become who we are called to be.

> Therefore, my brothers, I implore you by God's mercy to offer your very selves to him: a living sacrifice, dedicated and fit for his acceptance, the worship offered by mind and heart. Adapt yourselves no longer to the pattern of this present world, but let your minds be remade and your whole nature thus transformed. Then you will be able to discern the will of God, and to know what is good, acceptable, and perfect. (Rom. 12:1-2)

Questions for Reflection:

1. What has been my experience of church/Church? How has my experience changed through the years?

2. Has church been primarily a place where I attend liturgy? Has it been for me a community of believers? Has it been both?

3. What has been my rôle in the church? Has my rôle changed through the years? How?

4. How has daily meditation affected my experience of church/Church?

Application:

I will see when and where I think or speak of the church just as an institution, rather than as a Body in which I am a living part.

[78]

Christian discipleship is lived detachment and loving other-centredness. And meditation begins with a call that awakens us out of the coma of self-preoccupation. We are called, we are chosen. Meditation is our response to that call from the deepest centre of our awakened consciousness....

In meditation by letting go, by openness to the centre of being we learn how to love. (*The Heart of Creation*, p. 75)

Meditate for thirty minutes.

Prayer and community

This is the beginning of the First Letter of St John:

> It was there from the beginning; we have heard it; we have
> seen it with our own eyes; we looked upon it, and felt it
> with our own hands; and it is of this we tell. Our theme is
> the word of life. This life was made visible; we have seen it
> and bear our testimony; we here declare to you the eternal
> life which dwelt with the Father and was made visible to us.
> What we have seen and heard we declare to you, so that you
> and we together may share in a common life, that life which
> we share with the Father and his Son Jesus Christ. And we
> write this in order that the joy of us all may be complete.
>
> Here is the message we heard from him and pass on to
> you: that God is light, and in him there is no darkness at all.
> (1 John 1:1–5)

As we get further into this retreat we actually get closer to the
real beginning of our work. I want to start drawing things together.

Perhaps the greatest feature of St Benedict's Rule, and one that
is frequently ignored, is his confidence and joyous proclamation
that prayer and community are not opposed. In his vision they are
so interdependent as to be almost synonymous. Prayer, as I have
suggested to you, is in essence learning to pay attention to the
Other; and then to regard the Other not in a self-interested or self-
calculating way but simply for the Other's own sake, because in
fact the Other is infinitely lovable. In Benedict's vision God and
neighbour are not two entities clamouring for our attention at the
expense of the other. God does not demand our love at the

expense of our brother or sister. Indeed, love for one another is the deepening of our intrinsic communion with God rather than a dissipation of it. 'He who dwells in love is dwelling in God' (1 John 4:16). Similarly, the love we have for one another propels us deeper into the mystery of divine love itself. To love the God that we cannot see, we must love the brother or sister we can see. We can see our brother *as brother* precisely because we are convinced that God is our common source and goal, the *Father* of all.

To learn to pray as I have been suggesting requires a good deal of unlearning and can involve a good deal of suffering. If we are going to deepen our faith then we have to learn to leave behind us the prayers of our former life and enter into the deeper mystery of prayer. There is pain in the discovery that prayer is not a self-centred event but a self-transcending process in which we pass over to the other. We discover that prayer in this deeper sense of self-transcendence is an unimaginably enriching process because as we progress in prayer we learn to view all reality, and ourselves, no longer from our own limited viewpoint but from that of the Other. We begin to understand what St Paul meant when he said, 'the life I now live is not my life, but the life which Christ lives in me' (Gal. 2:20). In this experience, the pain of change and the pain of growth cannot be separated. Nor can they be compared with the glory we will discover within ourselves when we have the courage to become fully alive, fully alive in Christ. Remember those words of St Irenaeus: 'The glory of God is the human being fully alive.'

I think there comes a time in the life of every Christian when this challenge must be faced: a time when we have to choose decisively between the infantile prayer of the past – necessarily self-centred – and instead, to choose for the prayer of Jesus, the prayer that is going on within us, filling us with the life that takes us beyond ourselves – a life that shatters all the fear-laden barriers that have so far prevented us from being fully ourselves. It is because we are not fully ourselves that we are incapable of becoming fully brothers and sisters to one another. What distances us from our neighbour is our own fear. It is this fear that is cast out by the experience of the love of Christ active within us.

We have often heard it said in the past that prayer is a personal matter in which each person tries the various methods – as if there were really any 'methods' – and then chooses the one that suits him or her best. As I see it, prayer is the growing awareness of God in Jesus, and our personal prayer and our community prayer are just different aspects of the same growing awareness that we as individuals and as communities become more alive with the life of Christ. Unless we are convinced of this, our personal prayer can become a self-encapsulating process – as can community prayer and community life as well. A community can easily isolate itself from the outside world. If our Christian communities are not proclaiming the gospel with the sort of authority and enthusiasm that they should be, it must be because they are not praying; their prayer is not fulfilling this function of making them free men and women, free to proclaim the gospel of Jesus. Our communities must inspire others by breathing the Spirit into all who come into contact with us.

We must never settle for the inevitable deficiencies that sociologists tell us apply to all social groups. We are not just any gathering of people who got together to do any old job. We are the redeemed of Jesus Christ bound together in love, our hearts beating with the life of the Lord Jesus. We must understand that we are the elect, the anointed, the chosen of Jesus Christ. In other words, we must understand in all humility, and that means in reality, what is the nature of our Christian life and our commitment one to another. We are not setting out to achieve a psychological or sociological ideal. Our call is to be transformed and transfigured in Christ Jesus.

> Adapt yourselves no longer to the pattern of this present world, but let your minds be remade and your whole nature thus transformed. (Rom. 12:2)

[82]

This is why our prayer is central to grasping the full vigour and the full dimension of our Christian calling. We must never forget our sublime dignity as Christ's elect and anointed, which is always the dignity of being able to serve others. So our communities must become what we are called to be, each of them a fervent assembly of realized, fully conscious human beings, self-emptying disciples, self-transcending brothers and sisters, filled with the Spirit, the Spirit who is constantly praying in our hearts. This is the sign the world is looking for. They are not looking for boring conglomerations of like-minded, respectful automatons. They are looking for communities who are aware of the living and loving Lord Jesus in their midst. This is a marvellous calling. Why we are so slow and ineffective to put it into practice is a mystery.

How are we going to get out of this terrible under-self-evaluation? How are we going to proclaim the gospel? There is only one way: the way of prayer. We have got to be convinced – each one of us – that from now on we are going to pray in the length and height and depth of our spirit. This is a discovery we must make – an actual discovery of the prayer of the Spirit within our hearts. We must uncover what our unre-made minds keep covered up because the dis-covery of the prayer of the Spirit of Jesus within us teaches us that we can transcend all our own limitations. Of course we are limited human beings, but in Jesus those limitations are swept aside. If we can discover ourselves as the anointed, as the elect temples of the Holy Spirit, we will learn to reverence ourselves. We need not underestimate ourselves. We need not play down our calling, but look at it with reverence. In learning to reverence ourselves we learn to reverence others. We must love ourselves in order to love others. We must love all men and all women of all persuasions if we are to proclaim this gospel of love throughout the world. We must proclaim to all people that they are the anointed; that they are the holy temples of the Spirit of God.

I suggested earlier that in our prayer we let God *be*. We adore God as God is, all-holy, all-lovable, all-compassionate, all-forgiving.

[83]

We do not try to manipulate God. We let him be, as the One who cannot be manipulated, and in our prayer we bow in adoration. We do not cover God up with our clever words or empty formulas. We learn to worship from the depth of our spirit in silence and in awe. In our prayer, too, we learn to let our neighbour be. We learn not to try to manipulate other people, but to reverence and to love them just as we reverence and love the Lord our God. Because of this, prayer is the great school of responsible community. It is in and through prayer that we find the meaning of Christian community as the assembly of anointed brothers and sisters living with one another in profound, loving respect. Christian community is the experience of people living with those who are sensitively attuned one to the other on the wavelength of the same Spirit who has called each one to fullness of life. In others I recognize the same Spirit that lives in my own heart, the Spirit that constitutes my real self. In this recognition of the other person – the recognition which re-makes our minds – the other person comes into being as he or she really is. Then the real self of the other emerges, not just as a manipulated extension of my mind. When we recognize the Spirit in the other, the other moves and acts out of his or her own integral reality because they are no longer creatures of my imagination. Even if our ideas or principles clash we are held in unity by a mutual recognition of the essential reality in each other. The mutually supporting and suffering dynamic of Christ's mystical body has just this creative objective: that we help one another to realize our own essential being.

True community consists in the process whereby we each draw the other into the light of true being, each supporting one another in achieving our vocation of becoming the persons we are called to be. In this process we enter a deepening experience of the joyous quality of life as we discover the fullness of life in a loving faith shared with brothers and sisters. The prerequisite of this process is a mutual recognition of our own and of each other's infinite importance and infinite value. We possess this importance and value because we possess or are possessed by the indwelling Spirit of God which the glory and the power of Jesus has purchased for us. We see that these are present realities. Our capacity to experience and to respond to the reality of the other directly depends upon our capacity to let the other be. This otherness of others is essential for us to respect to if we want to understand who God is, if we want to understand who our neighbour is, and if we want to understand who we are.

There is something in all of us that wants to control the other, to diffuse the power we feel in the other and to protect ourselves from the transforming power of that feeling. What we then seek to do is to neutralize their otherness by imposing on it an identity which we fabricate. We are always getting people to conform to what *we* think we should be like and so we try to make others just like ourselves.

The sin of idolatry is to create our own God in our image and likeness. It is the deep fear of the other, particularly the incomprehensible otherness of God, that underlies so much of our timidity as we approach religious truths. We try to control God by our prayers and formulas rather than encountering God in his awesome difference from ourselves. We construct a toy model of God in our own psychic and emotional image. In doing so we debase and lose ourselves, surrendering the glory of our humanity for the likeness of a golden calf. But the truth is so much more marvellous than that. God is not a reflection of our narrow consciousness, but with our infinite potential to be realized we are the image and likeness of the God we worship. The call of the New Testament – the call of Jesus – is to the worship of this transcendent God who is totally Other from ourselves, the God who is life. It is the fear of otherness that causes us to go in for these cosy chats with God, making him a convenient shoulder to cry on.

The fear of otherness is one of the principal symptoms of alienation in our day. R. D. Laing in his book *The Divided Self* used the term implosion to describe the fear of the infringement of reality.

[85]

The individual feels that, like a vacuum, he is empty. But this emptiness is him. And although in other ways he longs for the emptiness to be filled he dreads the possibility of this happening because he has come to feel that all he can be is the awful nothingness of just this very vacuum. Any contact with reality is then itself experienced as a dreadful threat because reality as experienced from this position is necessarily implosive.

From these ideas we can see the reason for so much of the ineffectiveness of modern Christians. The experience that Laing describes here – the feeling of emptiness and even the sense of helplessness that accompanies it – is essentially a religious experience, for without God we *are* merely a vacuum. Perhaps we are even less than a vacuum. Perhaps we are the spiritual counterparts of the black holes in space that destroy and de-energize whatever enters them.

Christianity is a hope-filled response of the human heart when the human heart experiences itself as unreedeemed and unloved. The fullness of the Christian response is not a process of self-torturing or self-interrogation or self-analysis. The fullness of the Christian response is met in the person of Jesus Christ. Jesus as our redeemer, the one who saves us and the one who lives, the Risen Christ, delivers us from our narrowness, from our emptiness. It is in the person of Christ whom we encounter in our own hearts that we find the ultimate hope: the divine person of the Risen Lord Jesus. In meditation, as we learn to say the mantra with greater and greater fidelity, we go beyond ourselves and enter into the personhood of the Lord Jesus. So, as individuals and as communities, our calling is to transcend the limitations of our divided fear-ridden selves, and to open ourselves to the transforming and transfiguring reality in which we have our true being that is, the redemptive love of the Risen Lord Jesus.

Questions for Reflection:
1. What attitudes or principles distinguish the communities with which I am associated? How do they reflect my values?

2. How do John Main's insights into prayer, self-discovery and community resonate with aspects of my own life?

3. How can my practice of daily meditation help invigorate my life and my contribution to these communities?

4. How can I be Christ more faithfully in the circumstances of my life?

Application:
I will be more open to God's presence as Truth in my own life. I will look more closely for God as love in others and affirm the goodness of those around me, rather than judging them.

> The all-important aim in Christian meditation is to allow God's mysterious and silent presence within us to become more and more not only *a* reality, but *the* reality in our lives; to let it become that reality which gives meaning, shape and purpose to everything we do, to everything we are. (*Word Into Silence*, p. 3)

Meditate for thirty minutes.

Basic theology of Christian meditation

Therefore, now that we have been justified through faith,
let us continue at peace with God through our Lord Jesus
Christ, through whom we have been allowed to enter the
sphere of God's grace, where we now stand. Let us exult
in the hope of the divine splendour that is to be ours.
More than this: let us even exult in our present
sufferings, because we know that suffering trains us to en-
dure, and endurance brings proof that we have stood the
test, and this proof is the ground of hope. Such a hope is
no mockery, because God's love has flooded our inmost
heart through the Holy Spirit he has given us. (Romans
5:1–5)

In this last session of our retreat together, I want to try to give you
a summary of the basic theology of meditation. The first thing to
understand is the wonder and the marvel of silence. Silence has
always been felt as a path into the mystery of being. The Maitrya
Upanishad says:

There is something beyond our mind which abides in
silence in our mind. It is the supreme mystery beyond
thought and let one's mind and one's subtle body rest on
that and rest on nothing else.

In the Christian tradition St Ignatius of Antioch also understood the link between silence and reality: 'It is better to be silent
and real, rather than to talk and be unreal.' The purpose of meditation is to come to that ultimate reality which is beyond the

human mind. The great tragedy of our time is that we think that we will get everything by thinking. We in the Christian tradition are as bad as anyone in this, by defining Mass only as a rational creature. We have to learn be silent, to be filled with awe at what is above our rational mind, and so to worship. Worship is impossible without silence because once we come into the presence of the Mystery all we *can* do is bow and bend low.

Again I want to stress that the authority needed for the proclamation of the gospel is men and women of silence who speak out of the authority of their own experience; who speak of what they know. This authority can only be earned if we undertake the pilgrimage into silence and encounter, in the silence of our own spirit, the loving silence of the Lord Jesus.

For most modern people silence is a very threatening thing. It is very difficult for people to sit in silence. I remember years ago being out for a country walk with a friend of mine on a winter's afternoon and he said, 'Oh, there are some great friends of mine who live here, we'll call in and see them.' So we called in and an elderly couple welcomed us. We went into the drawing room and sat in front of the fire and they gave us a great welcome. Then we all sat in silence and looked into the fire. Not a word was spoken. And I thought, 'Good heavens, this is a queer lot.' After twenty minutes of this, the wife, with absolute relaxation said, 'What about a cup of tea?' Then she got up and made a cup of tea and everybody chatted. But there was a wonderful sense – I was unused to it, being about eighteen at the time – of people accepting one another and knowing that they were accepted. There was no compulsion to engage in small talk or anything. This silence is something we have to get used to work for. Again I urge you to consider the place of silence in your life. In our own meditation community we have been quite zealous in preserving silence in the house by controlling radios and televisions and talking in order to nurture our freedom. This is what meditation must bring us to: freedom, full liberty of spirit. What we are seeking to do is to unleash the power of God within us. To allow that power to have full play in our spirit.

When we begin to meditate, as you may know already from your experience, we have to face the amazing indiscipline of our mind that simply cannot be still. Our mind just hops away like a little child who has just been given a hoop to play with. It is there but we cannot control it. It goes whizzing around everywhere and we are trying to say our mantra thinking, 'It's impossible; I can't do it.' That is the first thing to face. You have to face the initial shame that you cannot control your own mind. As long as we cannot control it we cannot come to the deep silence within us because the din is too great. The mantra and its simplicity fulfills its first task: to bringing the surface areas of the mind into harmony with the deeper peacefulness within. That is the first and ongoing task of the mantra day by day.

The second task of the mantra is that once you have got those surface areas cleared, you do encounter – frequently, though not always – the darker side of your being where live the repressed fears and guilt feelings, things that we should not have done or, worse perhaps, things that we did not do and cannot do now because people have died or too much time has passed. Those fears and guilts and repressions can cause a lot of trouble. You just have to continue saying the mantra in a spirit of deep faith and let go of all that garbage and trivia. So I want to warn you. Do not be surprised in the early stages – that is, the first twenty years or so! – if you sometimes come from your meditation feeling anxiety, or less relaxed than you were when you began. Say the mantra and keep saying the mantra. This will free you from the inner bondage that prevents most people from praying with absolute freedom. It will free you from the chains of your repressed fears and anxieties that are the principal cause of distractions. This form of prayer is of immense importance, because it frees you from compulsions and the chains of guilt and fear.

I want to stress again that there is a risk involved in this pilgrimage to silence. It is a risk because it involves the whole of your being. You cannot just say, 'Well, okay. I'll try the mantra for a bit,' or, 'I'll try the mantra first thing in the morning and the last thing at night, but I'll be free to float the rest of the day.' Once you start to seek for the Lord Jesus in the depths of your being there is no alternative but to become willing to surrender your entire being to him. When you begin, it seems like nothing but surrender, nothing but giving. But as you progress through the spheres of silence, you encounter the light and the love of the Spirit of Jesus. You will quickly forget all the suffering, all the labour, all that has been involved in leading you to that light. And remember, we know that light is utterly beyond us and yet the present source of everything we are here and now. We put our entire trust in the Lord Jesus who calls us to leave all things and follow him. As we say the mantra we are, in fact, exploring the infinite depths of our poverty – poverty of mind and poverty of spirit. Then we come to experience our absolute dependence on God. Placing ourselves entirely in his arms we find the life that we surrendered restored to us a hundredfold. In fact, we find our life for the first time.

St Paul was able to cry, 'The life I now live is not my life, but the life which Christ lives in me' (Gal. 2:20). Paul's witness to Christ was a witness radiant with the risen life of the Lord, and the energy of that life was the source and the ground of his authority. We must all proclaim the gospel with the same authority – each of us in our unique way. Jesus has told us that we can only be followers of his if we leave self behind and take up our cross daily. Notice the word *daily*. Our *daily* meditation, then, is of paramount importance. It is something that we must learn to build into our lives – not with fanatacism – because we know that Jesus himself tells us to leave self behind daily.

We must be very honest with ourselves when we consider our calling as Christians. The utterness of the invitation of Christ, the total giving of himself, calls for a correspondingly total response from us. Christianity is not the sort of thing that we can fool around with: once we have understood the total commitment of Jesus Christ the Son of God to us, our only course of action is to commit ourselves. In understanding that, we come to understand our personal and total dedication to the demands and invitation of the gospel.

As we enter the silence within, we must understand that we are, quite literally, being *unmade*. St Paul, with good reason, constantly calls the response to Christian life a totally new creation, created out of the power of what Jesus has accomplished. And so, in accepting the invitation of Jesus to follow him, we accept the fact that the old self dies. The old self was crucified, in fact, with Christ. We are unmade. None of us can be the person we were or the person we thought we were. The invitation is much greater. It is to rise a new man or woman with Jesus. The wonder of the experience of prayer is that we are not being destroyed but unmade and remade. We are being awakened to the eternally fresh source of our being. Jesus speaks of 'an inner spring always welling up' (John 4:14). And that is what it is. Quite literally, it is the life of the Lord Jesus bubbling up within us. As André Louf puts it so beautifully:

> In our prayer we become aware that we are being created, that we are springing from the creator's hand and returning to him in his love. (*Teach Us to Pray*, Darton Longman & Todd)

It is that living quality of new life that is the experience of prayer. Jesus always points to the fact of our being alive with his life and returning with him to the Father.

So, in the silence, we are being prepared for a full awakening of spirit. Wakefulness is our encounter with the fullness and splendour of Jesus. Jesus is now in the fully alive state to which the resurrection awakened him. We must understand that it is not only the historical Jesus, who died, whom we encounter in our hearts; we encounter the Risen Lord, the Jesus whose last words were,

'It is accomplished.' And he then sent his Spirit forth. That is something that we have got to ponder deeply. The fully awakened Jesus, the fully powerful Jesus, the Jesus who sends us his Spirit to make all things new – he is the Lord we encounter in our hearts.

I must beware of allowing my own enthusiasm for meditation from misleading you about the perseverance that is required for the pilgrimage. But then listen to the New Testament telling us the splendour of the Lord Jesus Christ flooding our hearts. I have been saying all along that we have to read that book as if we have never read it before. Even if we know all this intellectually, we must be prepared for the process of suffering involved in meditation. Very often, what we experience to begin with is a shedding of qualities; a reduction not an expansion of spirit. We have to leave behind familiar paths, familiar ways of thinking. We move towards a poverty of spirit that can be extraordinarily threatening as we begin the pilgrimage, but we can overcome fear by learning to tread this path in simplicity and get used to *being* simple. In doing so, we have to follow Jesus all the way to Calvary. We have to, in his words, take up our cross daily. We do this, not in any self-dramatizing or self-obsessed way, but with joy knowing that we also rise with Jesus. We rise in his transcendent light, the light of the One who is completely free, who has passed beyond the veil we spoke of at the beginning of this retreat. To do that we must die with him, by dying to self. Paul puts it so beautifully: 'Though our outward humanity is in decay, yet day by day we are inwardly renewed' (2 Cor. 4:16). Notice again that with St Paul it is *day by day*. That is the capacity that the Christian must have for the daily taking up of the cross, the daily renewal, the daily rising with the Lord in the Spirit of light. As we persevere in our daily meditation we come to love and cherish those moments of stillness and silence as the most precious, most real moments of our day.

A guest came to see me late one night and asked if he could have a talk with me. We spoke a little but it was too late to talk much and I said, 'Why don't we just meditate together?' So we

[93]

did, for a half an hour, and afterwards he said to me, 'I don't think there can be a more beautiful way of spending a half an hour with another person.' That is what we come to understand. More can be accomplished in the shared silence than in all the talking in the world because we are being made new. Christ will make all things new. And as we enter these ever deeper centres of our own being we experience that harmony more and more fully. We experience the harmonious symphony of all the energies that are resolved at the centre which is the source of being: the most Holy Trinity. 'When anyone is united to Christ, there is a new world' (2 Cor. 5:17).

We have spoken before about the death and resurrection of Jesus as being the paradigm of all being. It is the great model on which each one of us must build our life: the dying to triviality, possessiveness and egoism; and the rising to that fullness of liberty of spirit where we find our true self created in the image and likeness of God and gaze upon him. As we continue to meditate we come to understand the great mystery that there is only one death and one resurrection, the death and resurrection of the Lord Jesus. We participate in his experience just as naturally as day follows night, as winter follows summer. The death-and-resurrection pattern is seen everywhere because it is the pattern that was based on the pattern of the Word through whom all things were made. There is only one death and one resurrection and we participate in it through everything the Lord underwent for all creation. This is something we must understand from our own experience, from the depths of our own being, not propositionally, not as a statement, but as experience. The Word proceeds from the silence of the Father and it returns to this unfathomable silence and limitless love of the Father. As William Blake did, we can see all this everywhere, infinitely, when we see with a pure heart. John Cassian and all the Desert Fathers presented the great aim and objective of meditation as purity of heart. Jesus said: 'How blest are those whose hearts are pure; they shall see God' (Matt. 5:8). We must understand and

[94]

never underestimate the profundity of our calling.

> In Christ he chose us before the world was founded, to be
> dedicated, to be without blemish in his sight, to be full of
> love; and he destined us – such was his will and pleasure –
> to be accepted as his sons [and daughters] through Jesus
> Christ, in order that the glory of his gracious gift, so gra-
> ciously bestowed on us in his Beloved, might redound to
> his praise. (Eph. 1:4–5)

The New Testament presents the staggering claim that our meaning is involved in the meaning of God Himself. To accept that – let
alone to understand it – we need purity of heart, simplicity of
being. There can be no place for egoism or complexity. We must
try to respond simply and then simply awaken. 'Unless you become like children you will never enter the kingdom of heaven.'

The aim of our meditation is to realize, to *make real*, our total
incorporation in Christ Jesus. For this we need attentiveness, simplicity and receptivity. We have to learn, not only to listen to the
silence within us, but to allow this cycle of returning to the Father
to be completed within us. The silence that I have been speaking
of is the silence that leads us to listen with Jesus who hears himself
eternally spoken by the Father.

Before we conclude this retreat, I want to put before you something that is almost totally incomprehensible. It is the experience
of Jesus awakening to himself, entering the spheres of silence within himself. And in finding his own Spirit he finds the source of his
Spirit: the Father. This is the self-same experience to which every
person born in the spirit is invited. Within the unimaginable design of the Father, we share that self-same experience.

The wonder of creation is not in a succession of awakenings
but the single, all-inclusive awakening to Jesus. It is to him, the
Lord of creation, fully awake in our own hearts, that we turn. And
he calls us to awaken us. Unfortunately, all language is quite in-
adequate to express this. Our minds are too puny to understand it.

[95]

But it is not language or the power of the mind, or anything of that sort, that we need. Our invitation as Christians is simply to become aware of the mysterious power of God within us. Once we realize it, this is what we have to lead others to. To approach this awakening, we need to be still, to be silent and to be attentive. The way that I know of, the path that I follow which leads to this, is the path of the one little word, the mantra.

Questions for Reflection:

1. 'It is better to be silent and real rather than to talk and be unreal.' Are there times when I talk just to hear myself talk? How can I show a deeper respect for shared silence?

2. Does silence enjoy an easeful presence in my daily life? If not, what adjustments can I make to better appreciate the gift of silence?

3. How can I accept the gift of meditation more completely? What changes must I make in my daily life to give a primary place to nurturing the practice of meditation, the reading of sacred Scripture and the service of others?

4. Why is it important to have a simple and non-possessive approach to meditation? Am I ready to cultivate those attitudes toward meditation while maintaining a strong commitment to the discipline?

Application:

I will recall, each day, my complete and utter dependence upon God for my life and my well-being. Daily meditation will open my heart to God's healing and creative presence.

As I have said before, if we Christians have a fault, it is that we are so blind to the extraordinary riches that are already ours, achieved for us, given to us by Jesus. We possess the mind of Christ – Christ who knows the Father and who knows us. This is what each of us is invited to discover from our own experience – that we know because we are known and that we love because we are loved ...

That is the invitation given to every one of us so that we may know personally from our own experience all that God of his own grace gives us. The way to that knowledge is the way of faithfulness, a daily faithfulness to our meditation. (*Moment of Christ*, p. 56)

Meditate for thirty minutes.

Book by John Main

Christian Meditation: The Gethsemani Talks. Medio Media, 1991.

Community of Love. Darton, Longman & Todd, 1990.

The Heart of Creation. Darton, Longman & Todd, 1988.

Letters from the Heart: Christian monasticism and the renewal of community. Crossroad, New York, 1982.

Moment of Christ. Darton, Longman & Todd, 1984.

The Present Christ. Darton, Longman & Todd, 1989.

The Way of Unknowing. Darton, Longman & Todd, 1980.

Word Into Silence. Darton, Longman & Todd, 1980.

Word Made Flesh. Darton, Longman & Todd, 1993.

The World Community
for Christian Meditation

Meditation in the tradition of the early Christian monks and as John Main passed it on has led to the formation of a world-wide community of meditators in over ninety countries. Weekly groups meet in many kinds of places and number over a thousand. An International Directory is maintained at the Community's London International Centre. A Guiding Board oversees the direction of the Community, a quarterly newsletter, the annual John Main Seminar, the School for Teachers, and the co-ordination of the Christian Meditation Centres around the world.

Medio Media

Founded in 1991, Medio Media is the publishing arm of the World Community for Christian Meditation. It is committed to the distribution of the works of John Main and many other writers in the field of contemplative spirituality and interfaith dialogue. Medio Media works in close association with the British publisher Arthur James. For a catalogue of books, audios, and videos contact Medio Media Ltd at the International Centre in London.

Christian Meditation Centres

International Centre

International Centre
The World Community for Christian Meditation
23 Kensington Square
London W8 5HN
Tel: 0171 937 4679
Fax: 0171 937 6790
e-mail: 106636.1512@compuserve.com

Australia

Christian Meditation Network
P.O. Box 6630
St Kilda Road
Melbourne, Vic. 3004
Tel: 03 989 4824
Fax: 03 525 4917

Christian Meditation Network
B.O. Box 323
Tuart Hill, WA 6060
Tel/Fax: 9 444 5810

Belgium

Christelijk Meditatie Centrum
Beiaardlaan 1
1850 Grimbergen
Tel: 02 269 5071

Brazil

Crista Meditacao Comunidade
CP 33266
CEP 22442-970
Rio de Janeiro RJ
Fax: 21 322 4171

Canada

Meditatio
P.O. Box 5523, Station NDG
Montreal, Quebec H4A 3P9
Tel: 514 766 0475
Fax: 514 937 8178

Centre de Méditation Chrétienne
Cap-Vie
367 Boulevard Ste-Rose
Tel: 514 625 0133

John Main Centre
470 Laurier Avenue, Apt 708
Ottawa, Ontario K1R 7W9
Tel: 613 236 9437
Fax: 613 236 2821

Christian Meditation Centre
10 Maple Street
Dartmouth, N. S. B2Y 2X3
Tel: 902 466 6691

India

Christian Meditation Centre
1/1429 Bilathikulam Road
Calicut
673006 Kerala
Tel: 495 60395

Ireland

Christian Meditation Centre
4 Eblana Avenue
Dun Laoghaire, Co. Dublin
Tel: 01 280 1505

Christian Meditation Centre
58 Meadow Grove
Blackrock, Cork
Tel: 021 357 249

Italy

Centro di Meditazione Cristiana
Abbazia di San Miniato al Monte
Via Delle Porte Sante 34
50125 Firenze
Tel/Fax: 055 2476302

New Zealand

Christian Meditation Centre
P.O. Box 35531
Auckland 1310

Philippines

5/f Chronicle Building Cor. Tektite Road
Meralco Avenue / Pasig
M. Manila
Tel: 02 633 3364
Fax: 02 631 3104

Singapore

Christian Meditation Centre
9 Mayfield Avenue
Singapore 438 023
Tel: 65 348 6790

Thailand

Christian Meditation Centre
51/1 Sedsiri Road
Bangkok 10400
Tel: 271 3295

United Kingdom

Christian Meditation Centre
29 Campden Hill Road
London W8 7DX
Tel/Fax: 0171 912 1371

Christian Meditation Centre
13 Langdale Road
Sale, Cheshire M33 4EW
Tel: 0161 976 2577

Christian Meditation Centre
Monastery of Christ the King
Bramley Road
London N14 4HE
Tel: 0181 449 6648
Fax: 0181 449 2338

Christian Meditation Centre
29 Mansion House Road
Glasgow
Scotland G41 3DN
Tel: 0141 649 4448

United States

John Main Institute
7315 Brookville Road
Chevy Chase, MD 20815
Tel: 301 652 8635

Christian Meditation Centre
1080 West Irving Park Road
Roselle, IL 60172
Tel/Fax: 630 351 2613

Christian Meditation Centre
322 East 94th Street No. 4B
New York, NY 10128
Tel: 212 831 5710

Christian Meditation Centre
2321 South Figueroa Way
Los Angeles, CA 90007-2501

Christian Meditation Centre
1619 Wight Street
Wall, NJ 07719
Tel: 908 681 6238
Fax: 908 280 5999

Christian Meditation Centre
2490 18th Avenue
Kingsburg, CA 93631
Tel: 209 897 3711

Hesed Community
3745 Elston Avenue
Oakland, CA 94602
Tel: 415 482 5573

Meditation on the Internet

WCCM.Archives
The WCCM, in collaboration with the Merton Research Institute
(Marshall University, USA), has archived a number of files: how to meditate; biographical information on John Main, Laurence Freeman, and
others; International Newsletters; catalogues of books, audiotapes, and
videotapes; the Rule of St Benedict and Benedictine oblates; the International Calendar of events; John Main Seminars; New Testament
sources; and more. The Index of files and all individual files may be

retrieved by anonymous FTP or the WWW using the following URLs:

> ftp://mbdu04.redc.marshall.edu/pub/merton/wccm/
> http://www.marshall.edu/~stepp/vri/merton/wccm.html

The URLs for the Merton Archives are:

> ftp://mbdu04.redc.marshall.edu/pub/merton/
> http://www.marshall.edu/~stepp/vri/merton/merton.html

Merton-L is a forum for discourse on contemplative life. To subscribe, send e-mail to

> listserv@wvnvm.wvnet.edu

containing the single line of text:

> subscribe merton-l yourname

(substituting your real name for yourname, of course).

WCCM Forum

The WCCM.Forum is an outgrowth of the WCCM.Archives. Again, in collaboration with the Merton Research Institute, the expressed and sole purpose of the WCCM.Forum is to provide a place for substantive discussion on the daily practice of Christian Meditation as taught by John Main, the works of John Main and Laurence Freeman, and the work of the WCCM in general.

T6: WCCM, John Main, Laurence Freeman

In keeping with the expressed purpose of the WCCM.Forum as described above, posts about other types of meditation should not be posted to the T6 channel of Merton-L. (See the Merton-L faq for information about discussions on other channels.) Posts to T6 are moderated by the Merton-L owner(s) and are also monitored by T6 discussion leader, Gregory Ryan, who is the archivist of the WCCM electronic files. Questions or comments of a personal nature or suggestions concerning T6 may be submitted to Greg via e-mail:

> gjryan@aol.com.

To subscribe to T6

To join the channel one must be a present member of Merton-L or, if not, subscribe to it. To subscribe to Merton-L, send e-mail to

listserv@wvnvm.wvnet.edu

containing the following single line of text:

subscribe merton-l yourname

(substituting your real full name for yourname, of course). Anyone who has subscribed to Merton-L may join the WCCM channel by sending e-mail to

listserv@wvnvm.wvnet.edu

(from your subscription address) containing the following single line of text:

set merton-l topics: +T6

Also in this series:

The Mystery Beyond

In this retreat, **Bede Griffiths**, one of the great spiritual forces of this
century, guides us to a deeper insight into the reality of our spiritual
quest. He addresses the dangers of fundamentalism and intolerance in
all religious traditions and shows how meditation opens us to the
transcendent unity of the non-dual – where we are ourselves but know
ourselves to be one with all others. In the light of this experience he
goes on to reveal his exciting and prophetic understanding of the
church and its purpose in the world.

Bede Griffiths (1907–93) is recognised by leaders in all religious
traditions as one of the prophets of the twentieth century. A
Benedictine monk, he left England to spend the last forty years of his
life in India where, he said, 'he discovered the other half of my soul'.
His autobiography *The Golden String* and his later book *The
Marriage of East and West* show how truly he pursued his call to be a
bridge between spiritual traditions.

'The whole of humanity constitutes in principle the mystical Body
of Christ … but the Christian revelation does not deny that the divine
mystery is present in different modes, different expressions, different
symbols, different languages in different parts of the world.'

Also in this series:

Aspects of Love

In this retreat **Laurence Freeman** explores the central value of all essential spiritual life. Love matters to us all. But what does it mean and how can I learn to love – and to allow myself to be loved. Love of self, of others and of God: these are the Aspects of Love which Laurence Freeman describes as our way of experiencing the simplicity and richness of love. He offers simple but surprising insights into how we can enter love's reality more wholly.

Laurence Freeman is a Benedictine monk of the Monastery of Christ the King, London, and Director of The World Community for Christian Meditation, a global contemplative network inspired by the teachings of John Main.

'What finally heals the wounds of self-division is love. Love unifies, unites and overcomes the wounds of our alienation and simplifies us.'

Also in this series:

Self and Environment

Writing from his hermitage in the forests of British Columbia, **Charles Brandt** leads us in this retreat to a fuller sense of the sacredness of creation and of our oneness with nature. He explores the damage inflicted on our sense of self and of God by the split we have made between humanity and the natural world. He helps us recover wholeness by showing how meditation and insight into the beauty of the world offer vital hope for a world in crisis.

Charles Brandt was trained as an ornithologist and environmentalist before being ordained as a hermit priest in British Columbia. He occasionally leads retreats which share the fruit of his solitude.

'My hermitage is located deep in the temperate rain forest on the Oyster River. The logging road along with other trails through the forest is where I practice walking meditation. I do not think of the road as leading anywhere. It is the road to nowhere, the path on which I journey and have been journeying for a lifetime ...'

Also in this series:

Silent Wisdom, Hidden Light

Eileen O'Hea's experience as a psychotherapist and as a spiritual guide for individuals and communities makes her an inspiring and refreshing voice of wisdom for this retreat. Exploring meditation as a way to the transformation of our minds, she recognizes – and helps to defuse – many of the fears, inner blocks and negative self-understanding which often prevent us from coming to our full potential.

Eileen O'Hea is a therapist and spiritual teacher, born in New York and now living in Minnesota. She serves on the Guiding Board of The World Community for Christian Meditation and is the author of *Woman: Her Intuition for Otherness* and many articles.

'The spiritual awakening of an individual is a process in which the person can no longer identify their sense of self with the world of the ego.'